Sidney Oldall Addy

Household Tales with other Traditional Remains

Collected in the Counties of York, Lincoln, Derby, and Nottingham

Sidney Oldall Addy

Household Tales with other Traditional Remains
Collected in the Counties of York, Lincoln, Derby, and Nottingham

ISBN/EAN: 9783337070762

Printed in Europe, USA, Canada, Australia, Japan

Cover: Foto ©ninafisch / pixelio.de

More available books at **www.hansebooks.com**

HOUSEHOLD TALES

TRADITIONAL REMAINS

*Collected in the Counties of York, Lincoln, Derby,
and Nottingham*

BY

SIDNEY OLDALL ADDY, M.A. Oxon.,

AUTHOR OF

"THE SHEFFIELD GLOSSARY" (ENGLISH DIALECT SOCIETY), "THE HALL OF WALTHEOF," ETC.

DAVID NUTT IN THE STRAND

PAWSON AND BRAILSFORD

1895

TABLE OF CONTENTS

TRADITIONAL REMAINS.

INTRODUCTION.

I.—HOUSEHOLD TALES.

THE fifty-two short stories printed in this volume have been got together during the last six or seven years. A deluge of cheap literature has fallen upon us since the days when the brothers Grimm made their famous German collection, and the memory, assisted by books, is apt to forget the unwritten lore. But still the ancient stories, beautiful or highly humorous even in their decay, linger with us here and there in England, and, like rare plants, may be found by those who seek them. Though some of the stories here printed illustrate the poverty of present tradition, it is likely that others were never told at greater length, or in better form.

In every case I have either written the tales down from dictation, or a written copy has been given to me. I have added nothing except the occasional formula, "Once upon a time," or a title to a story which had no title. Nor have I taken anything away. As nearly as I could manage it, the tales are given in the very words of the narrators. I have hardly attempted to reproduce dialect, but obsolete words, when used by the narrator, have been retained. And when the narrator has used such a word as "mamma," I have not hesitated to write "mother." The tales have all been obtained from oral tradition, and not from printed sources. Many more of them must be embedded in the memories of the people, but the collection of these things usually falls to the lot of those who are otherwise busy.

A few remarks on the scope of the tales, and the lessons which they teach to the archæologist, seem necessary.

It will be seen that witchcraft is very prominent in our tales, and it will appear that gifts were made to witches to obtain their favour and assistance in the ordinary affairs of life. In one story a boy who will not give butter-milk to a witch is threatened with boiling alive. In another story we are told that a farmer and his wife have been accustomed to give butter-milk to a witch. One day the farmer's daughter refuses to give the butter-milk, and after that butter will not come in the churn. In another story a farmer tells his men never to refuse to give anything that a witch might ask of them. But one of the men refuses her request, after which his horses will not go. In another story the horses of a carter who refuses to give the witch a pipe of tobacco are bewitched, and will not move on. Here we have four tales, derived from independent sources, in which the leading idea is that gifts ought to be offered to the witch, just as bowls of cream are offered to the fairies or local deities.* And as regards the pipe of tobacco, let us not forget that offerings made to the fairies had by no means ceased when tobacco was first brought into England.

It is not unlikely that the numerous small tobacco pipes to which the name of "fairy pipes" has been given, and which are so often found upon or near to old earthworks, were intended as gifts to the fairies, otherwise the local deities or spirits of the dead. Two or three centuries ago belief in fairies and witchcraft was very strong in the minds of the English people, and the ancient notion that the dead needed the comforts and consolations of the living may have led to pious and secret offerings to them of little pipes of tobacco. I do not know any other way of accounting for the presence of these "fairy pipes" upon old mounds. It may be said, indeed, that they came from the ash-

* Amongst the Norsemen, sibyls or spae-wives, according to the popular fancy, went about the land and told men their fates. For this they received presents.

pit or refuse heap along with the manure which was laid on the land. But this explanation will not account for their presence on lands which are not enclosed or cultivated. " Small tobacco pipes," says Mr. Croker in his *Fairy Legends and Traditions of the South of Ireland,* " of an ancient form, are frequently found in Ireland on digging or ploughing up the ground, particularly in the vicinity of those circular entrenchments, called Danish forts, which were more probably the villages or settlements of the native Irish. These pipes are believed by the peasantry to belong to the Cluricaunes, and when discovered are broken, or otherwise treated with indignity, as a kind of retort for the tricks which their supposed owners had played off."[*] The Rev. R. A. Gatty has found these pipes at Bradfield, near Sheffield. He describes them as "pigmy pipe bowls," and says that he has found them in the ploughed fields. "I have picked up," he says, " from time to time, upwards of a hundred specimens, when looking for flint implements. They vary a little in design, and sometimes makers' marks are found on the spur under the bowl."[†] In a letter to me Mr. Gatty says: " You never find them whole in the stem, except when behind old wainscots in very old houses. . . . . I found a hundred or more on the moorside at Bradfield. Who smoked up there in those days ? . . . . . The fairies are supposed to smoke, but where they get their tobacco from is a secret. Certainly the pipes are quite small enough for such small folk, and I have some specimens quite absurd in size. I am certain that the people believed in the fairies smoking. My old clerk at Bradfield—who always swore by the *mess*, not mass—used to argue the point with a friend over a glass of beer." Now there is a close resemblance between these gifts to witches and offerings made to the spirits of the dead. Accordingly the pipe of tobacco demanded by the witch in our tale resembles the offering made to the fairy or disembodied spirit inhabiting the hill or the ancient mound. And, as we shall presently see, the witch and the fairy are identical.

---

[*] Quoted from Hone's *Table Book*, 1827, ii., p. 771.
[†] Gatty's *A Life at One Living*, 1884, p. 213.

Mr. W. F. Jackson has lent me a small pipe bowl found in a field near Bailey Hill, in Bradfield, in 1887. It is made of white pipe-clay, and might very well have been made 250 years ago. It is worn at the edges, and the stem has been broken off sharply at its junction with the bowl; the aperture leading into the bowl remains. There is no spur, and the bowl is flattened beneath. A dotted line has been made round and near the edge of the bowl by way of ornament. The outside depth of the bowl is an inch and a quarter, the inside depth fifteen-sixteenths of an inch. The diameter of the bowl, measured from the outside, is half an inch. I found by experiment that the bowl of a modern tobacco pipe, of average size, would hold three times as much as this little bowl. I regard it as a specimen of the ordinary tobacco bowl once made in England, and not as having been specially made for the fairies, as bad money is manufactured for the gods in China.*

Even in England money is offered to the gods when a shilling is put into the churn to make the butter come.†

Mr. Hartland has arrived at the conclusion that no positive distinction can be made between ghosts and witches and fairies. "Whether," he says, "it be child-stealing, transformation, midnight meetings, possession and gift of enchanted objects, spell-binding, or whatever function, or habit, or power be predicted of one, it will be found to be common to the three. I conclude, therefore, that they are all three of the same nature. This is what a consideration of the superstitions of savages would lead me to expect. The belief in fairies, ghosts, and witches is a survival of those superstitions."‡ Before Mr. Hartland had published his book my own observations had led me to a similar conclusion. Not the least forcible of the reasons which led me to entertain this view was the statement made to me by an old Derbyshire man, and recorded in a subsequent part of this volume, that "fairies are always dressed in a red mantle and

* See an article in the *Times* of November 11, 1893, entitled "Cheating the Gods."

† See p. 81.

‡ *The Science of Fairy Tales*, 1891, p. 348.

hood which covers the whole body, and witches are dressed exactly in the same manner." Witches, like fairies, are the spirits of the dead.

In Dead Lane, or Deadman's Lane, at Ecclesall, near Sheffield, "a headless woman, robed in white," is still believed to wander by night. Are not these "headless women," who occur so often in popular tradition, the dead wandering about in their grave clothes, and is not the hood or mantle the shroud? A form so dressed would appear headless, and the fairy dressed in "a red mantle and hood, which covers the whole body," seems to be nothing more than a dead man in his shroud. In Eyrbyggia Saga Thorgunna's body was "swathed in linen, but not sewn up, and then laid in the coffin."* There is a Middle High German word *hächel*, Dutch *hecksel*, which means a witch, and with this word we may compare the Old Norse *hökull*, meaning a priest's cope or mantle, Old English *hacela*, Old High German *hachul*. And then we have the Old Norse *hekla*, a cowled or hooded frock. So that the Old Norse *hökull* appears to have developed the following meanings :

1. A cope or hooded frock.
2. A dead body habited in a long robe.
3. A witch or fairy so habited.

Again, we have the Old Norse *grima*, a hood, and Grímr, a name of Odin. All this is easy to understand when we bear in mind that the gods are themselves spirits, or dead men's ghosts.

According to the beliefs once held it would seem quite natural that the dead should wander about in their grave clothes. We also learn from the present collection that they carried bags or provision bags with them. This is apparent from the bag of nuts buried under the dead woman's head,† coupled with the tale in which a witch or disembodied spirit threatens to put "Jack" into her bag.‡ The Old Lad or Devil is also said to carry a nutting-bag with him. In the tale of "The Little Watercress Girl" the witch has a white bag. Now just as

---

* Chapter 51.   † P. 4.   ‡ P. 7.

Hächel meant both mantle and fairy—for witches and fairies are identical—so Puck or Poake* (poke) meant both bag and fairy. We learn, then, that it was once a common practice to bury bags containing provisions, such as nuts, for the dead. And this is consistent with the well-known discoveries of food and "food-vessels" in English barrows. In the Edda Thialfi carries Thor's bag (*kýl*) or provision bag (*nest-baggi*), and, in the Tale of Thridrandi, Thorhall says, "I laugh because many hills open, and every soul, both small and big, packs up his bag (*býr sinn bagga*) and makes flitting-day of it." Here the dead are coming out of their howes, each with his bag.

In our tales trees and animals speak. "The Wizard of Lincoln" changes himself into a blackbird and speaks as such. In one tale a hawk, a parrot, and a ploughman talk to each other as though they were all human.† In another very remarkable story‡ a girl asks an old apple-tree to hide her from a witch whose bag of money she has stolen, and the witch asks every tree in the orchard if it has seen the girl. In a third tale§ a girl talks to two robins, or robinets, as they are called in Derbyshire, who advise her to stuff her sieve with moss and daub it with clay when she fetches water therein from a well. In the tale of "The Glass Ball" a horse, a cow, and other animals are made to speak. From such tales we may infer that our ancestors, like savages, once regarded all things—trees, birds, stones, in short, everything animate and inanimate—as equally conscious with themselves and possessed of some power of reasoning. If we compare these traditional remains with similar remains in countries far beyond the British seas, and if we also compare our English folk-lore with the beliefs of modern savages, we shall be forced to the conclusion that Great Britain was once inhabited by men whose condition can only be described as a condition of savagery.

* Keightley's *Fairy Mythology*, 1889, p. 317.
† "The Hawk and the Parrot," No. 11.
‡ "The Little Watercress Girl," No. 10.
§ "The Girl who fetched Water in a Riddle," No. 39.

In four of our tales the fairies appear as the friends and guides of mankind. They help the distressed and needy, and by gentle reprimand point out error and wrong, and show the better way. The children of a poor widower are washed and dressed, and his bread is baked by them. When a brother abandons his dead sister's child the fairies pull the clothes off his bed every night until he takes the child into his care. Even so venial an offence as gossiping meets with their rebuke, for when a grandmother having the care of her dead daughter's child goes out gossiping, the fairies, to show their sense of the danger in which the child might be, take it out of bed, though the door is locked, and dress it in its mother's clothes. A younger brother who has disagreed with his elder brother is admonished by the fairies amidst sounds of music to leave his elder brother's house and build a house elsewhere. In these last-mentioned tales the voice of the fairy is as the voice of conscience—a power which is stronger than all the courts of law and equity. The law will not compel a man to maintain his dead sister's children, and will not punish a woman who goes gossiping and neglects her house. But the fairies sit in the high court of conscience, and provide a remedy for wrongs which are beyond the reach of human law. They lead the wrong-doer to do right by mild persuasion. Men who are not amenable to human judgments dare not disobey the gentle voice of the spirit.

In the tale of "The Minister and the Fairies" the good priest—who appears in the modern guise of a Methodist minister—is invited to a supper prepared for "beautiful men and women," who represent fairies, or spirits of the dead. The point of the story consists in the minister's refusal of the food of the dead. He had entered the place of the dead, and had he tasted their food he could never have returned to the land of the living. "The Nuts and the Sheep," as I have observed in a footnote to that story, occurs in "A Hundred Merry Tales" and in other ancient books. It was evidently very popular in the Middle Ages, not only in England but in other parts of Europe.

This tale was told to me by a poor workman who could barely read, who could not write at all, and who possessed neither books nor access to books. I am certain that it had come down to him, without any help from books, from a distant antiquity. The tale is highly ludicrous, and the joke is at the expense of a parson and his sexton.   My informant has preserved the incident of the " bag of nuts."   In the version given in " A Hundred Merry Tales " a rich husbandman makes his executor promise to bury a bag of nuts in his grave, and a miller goes the night after to fetch them out. In our version a young man goes to fetch a bag of nuts which lies beneath his dead mother's head in the churchyard. Did he want to show how brave he could be, and what little fear he had of ghosts, or is the bag of nuts introduced to make the tale as horrible and ludicrous as possible ? Or is it an accidental survival of some long-forgotten custom, such as the burying of nuts with a dead man to provide food for him in the next world ? We shall see that in Derbyshire food is still placed beside the dead.* Vessels containing the remains of food for the dead are found in ancient burial mounds on the Yorkshire wolds.† Mr. Hartland thinks that " the food buried with the dead by uncivilised tribes may be meant to provide them against the contingency of having to partake of the hospitality of the Shades, and so afford them a chance of escaping back to the upper air."‡ It was an old belief that unless a man refused the food of the dead, he would remain with them for ever. We are told in Gill's *Myths and Songs of the South Pacific* how a man " directed that, as soon as the breath was out of his body, a cocoa-nut should be cracked, and its kernel disengaged from the shell and placed upon his stomach under the grave-clothes." By stealthily eating the cocoa-nut instead of the disgusting food offered to him in Hades he managed to return to the upper world.§ Doubtless the nuts under the dead mother's head in our tale, like the peas and wheat found in Egyptian mummy cases, were put there for a similar purpose,

---

* P. 123.   † Greenwell's *British Barrows, passim.*
‡ *Science of Fairy Tales*, 1891, p. 47.
§ Quoted by Mr. Hartland, *ut supra*, p. 45.

and the son who ate them would take away her only chance of
returning to life.

The belief that giants, or other supernatural beings, were the
makers and builders of great earthworks or stoneworks, such as
ancient walls or roads, and the dikes about which so little is
known, is apparent in one of our tales,* and also in another
part of this book.† We have already seen how the fairies help
man in his troubles and difficulties, and one of our tales will
show how Hob Thurst, the friend of peasants, is ever ready at
need. The invisible being who mowed the farmer's hay for
him in the night, or made an incredible number of shoes for
the cobbler, could accomplish greater works than these. In
the tale called " The Devil's Ditch " a road is made by a name-
less invisible being, who tells a horseman to ride in the direction
that he would have the road to go, and the road is made behind
the horseman as he rides. But, just as in the case of Lot's wife,
or Orpheus, his desire to do the forbidden thing overcomes him,
and he looks back. Then the road stops, and in the place where
the horseman turned round may be seen not a pillar of salt but
a great ditch called "the Devil's Ditch," which can never be
filled up to this day. A similar account is given of a road
near Crowle, in Lincolnshire, which was made by the fairies
and never can be finished, because a farmer could not resist
the desire to turn round and see how the road-making was
done.‡

It is very likely that folk-tales were distributed in England
by wandering pedlars, tinkers, and merchants, many of whom
came from foreign lands. I have dealt with this subject in
another place,§ but I might here refer to the Old Norse *um-
renningr*, the land-louper who went from house to house dis-
tributing news and tales, and in short performing the office of a
walking newspaper and story book.‖ A little story in this
collection, called " The Endless Tale," which mentions locusts,
has all the extravagance of Oriental imagination.

---

* No. 26.   † P. 135.   ‡ P. 135.
§ *Hall of Waltheof*, 1893, p. 215, *seq.*
‖ See Vigfusson and Powell's *Icelandic Reader*, pp. 218, 409.

The "Jack Otter" of our tale"* is plainly Höttr or Odin, and had not the Old Norse word been here preserved he would have been called "Jack Hood." The mention of this name has led me to look into the ballads about Robin Hood, and to enquire whether he and his companions are not the gods Odin, Loki, and Honir, including, perhaps, Thor. I would suggest that—

    1. Robin Hood = Höttr, Hood, or Deep Hood, *i.e.* Odin.
    2. Scathelocke = Loki.
    3. Little John = Honir.
    4. Much the miller's son† = Thor?

In Völsunga Saga, Odin, Loki, and Honir are represented as going about in the world, like men in search of adventure; and in the Eddic legend these same three gods go from home, over the hills, and across the wilderness. They come down into a dale where a herd of oxen are feeding, and, like freebooters, take an ox and seethe it.

The name Scathelocke may stand for an Old Norse word Scaða-loki, like skaða-maðr, killer, slayer, and as regards the compound we may compare Útgarða-loki. In the Edda we are told that Loki cut Sif's hair off, for which Thor threatens to break every bone in his body. And hence we find him described as hárskaði Sifjar. And then Scaða-loki would suit his well-known character as the foe of the gods, although he was their companion, and especially would it be suitable to him in his character of the destroyer of Balder. Negative evidence in favour of this opinion would be found in the non-existence of such a surname as Scathelocke, and I have not been able to find it. Moreover, the names of Robin Hood's companions, such as Reynold Greenleaf, are all fanciful or mythical. The name Loki seems to occur in Loxley, near Sheffield, for Lock or Lok may be inferred from Scathe-lock. *Locs-leáh* would be a very appropriate name for a rocky, untilled place such as Loxley was till late years, and, like Canon Atkinson's *Moorland Parish*

---

* No. 8.
† *Much* may be used in the old sense of "tall." Miller's son = *mellu-sonr*, son of the giantess, *i.e.* Earth?

—" the devil of a country." For who but a fiend could have made it?

With regard to Little John, the evidence is of less weight, on account of the prefix "Little." But it is remarkable that we should have traditions about his tall stature. He is said to have been "seven foot high" in a late ballad printed by Ritson.* At Hathersage, in Derbyshire, the people still point out his grave in the village churchyard, and say that he was a very tall man. In the last century, Wilson, the Sheffield antiquary, wrote: " His grave is distinguished by two small stones set up at each end, and is four yards ten inches long betwixt stone and stone."† Now, according to Vigfusson and Powell, the god Honir or Hœne is described in phrases taken from lost poems as *langi fótr*, or the long-legged one; and as *aur-konungr*, the lord of the ooze. " Strange epithets," they say, " are these, but easily explainable when one gets at the etymology of Hœne = hohni = Skt. sakunas = Gk. cúcnos = the white bird, swan, or stork, that stalks along in the mud, lord of the marish—and it is now easy to see that this bird is the Creator walking in Chaos, brooding over the primitive mish-mash or tohu-bohu, and finally hatching the egg of the world." ‡

There is one thing in a ballad about Robin Hood which, to me at least, is puzzling, viz. the place called " the Sayles." Thus in the " fourth fytte " we have:

> Take thy bowe in hande, sayd Robyn,
> Let Moch wende with the,
> And so shall Wyllyam Scathelock,
> And no man abide with me,

> And walke up into the Sayles
> And to Watlynge-strete,
> And wayte after 'some' unketh gest,
> Up-chaunce ye may them mete

* * * * *

* ii. 21.
† In Bateman's *Ten Years' Diggings*, p. 251.
‡ *Corpus Poeticum Boreale*, i. p. cii. And see *Edda* (*Skaldskaparmál*), Egilsson's ed., p. 56.

> They went up to the Sayles,
> These yemen all thre ;
> They loked est, they looked west,
> They myght no man se.

As to the word " Sayles " * in this poem, is it not possibly the same place as the Lith-shelf of Northern mythology, the place from which the gods looked down on the world ? " On a day," says the Edda, " Freyr had gone to Lith-shelf, and beheld therefrom all the world. As he searched in the northern region he saw a great and fair house, and to the house went a woman," &c.† And of the place called Himinbjörg, or the Heavenly Mountains, the Edda says, " There is a mighty abode called Wala-shelf ; that place Odin has, and the gods made it, and thatched it with shining silver, and there in that hall is Lith-shelf, the high seat which is so called, and when the Father of All sits in that seat he beholds all the world."‡ The mention of Watling Street immediately after " the Sayles " makes this inference more probable, a heavenly, and not an earthly, way being intended. " The starry street in the night sky is known as the *spirit-path* to many savage tribes, and perhaps even to our forefathers (as the Editor's countryman, Mr. Gisli Brynjulfsson, has suggested) ' Vættlinga stræt.' "§

Amongst the earliest recollections of my childhood is the performance of the " Derby Ram," or, as we used to call it, the Old Tup. With the eye of memory I can see a number of young men standing one winter's evening in the deep porch of an old country house, and singing the ballad of the Old Tup. In the midst of the company was a young man with a sheep's skin, horns and all, on his back, and standing on all fours. What it all meant I could not make out, and the thing that most impressed me was the roar of the voices in that vault-like

---

* Is it not the O. N. *salr*, hall, as in *Srölnis salr*, Walhall, *Óðins salr*, Odin's hall, &c. ? In Old Norse poetry there are many figures and metaphors for the sky compounded with this word, as for instance *röðla-salr*, star hall, or heavenly vault, *berg-salr*, mountain hall or sky.

† Egilsson's ed., Reykjavik, 1848, p. 22.

‡ *Ibid.*, p. 12.

§ Vigfusson and Powell's *C. B. P.*, i. 420.

porch. The sheep and the men were evidently too harmless to frighten any child, and a play in which the only act was the pretended slaughter of an old tup was not in itself attractive. I remember the following lines:

> As I was going to Darby, all on a market day,
> I met the finest tup, sir, that ever was fed with hay.
>> Fay lay, fay lay, folderol, older, I day.

> This tup was fat behind, sir, this tup was fat before,
> This tup was ten miles high, sir, indeed he was no more.
>> Fay lay, &c.

> The wool that grew on his back, sir, it was so mighty high.
> The eagles built their nesses * in't, for I heard the young ones cry.
>> Fay lay, &c.

> The butcher that stuck this tup, sir, was up to the eyes in blood,
> And all the old women in Darby were washed away by the flood.
>> Fay lay, &c.

Then the ballad went on to tell how and for what purpose people begged for his bones, eyes, teeth, hide, &c., but I cannot remember more of it. However, in a version printed by Jewitt,† they beg for his horns to make milking pails, and for his eyes to make footballs. And a tanner begs for his hide, which is big enough "to cover all Sinfin Moor." Here we have a ballad describing the slaughter of a being of monstrous size, and the uses to which his body was put. Now when I first read the Edda, and came to the passage which tells how the sons of Bor slew the giant Ymir, and how, when he fell, so much blood ran out of his wounds that all the race of frost-giants was drowned in it, I said to myself, "Why, that's the Old Tup"! and when I read further on and found how they made the sea from his blood, the earth from his flesh, the rocks from his teeth, the heaven from his skull, it seemed to me that I had guessed rightly. The Old Tup was the giant Ymir, and the mummers of my childhood were acting the drama of the Creation.

---

* Nests. † *Derbyshire Ballads*, 1867, p. 115.

II.—TRADITIONAL REMAINS.

I T is not pretended that every superstitious belief or practice included under this heading in the following pages is of great antiquity. For example, the belief that it is unlucky for a clock to stand opposite a fire cannot be older than the invention of clocks. Great as is the age of many of these superstitious beliefs, it must not be forgotten that the formation of such beliefs still goes on in the untaught or undeveloped mind. But whether these conceptions be of primitive origin, or of more recent growth, they form part of a barbarous philosophy. In the main they are the long-descended survivals of ideas which the ancestors of the English people held in common with races, now inhabiting the earth, whose evolution from barbarism has progressed more slowly than our own. They may be included under the modern word folk-lore, which a writer in the *Quarterly Review* has defined as " the geology of the human race."

It may be well to examine briefly a few of the superstitious beliefs and practices recorded in this volume, mainly in the hope of learning something about the early condition of man in Great Britain.

When an English peasant is told by a friend that his ill luck is owing to his having forgotten to bow to the new moon, we have evidence not only of a belief in the efficacy of the moon in influencing human destiny, but also of the existence of moon-worship.

I have not met with any instance of actual sun-worship, though the luminary whose name appears in Sun-day must once have claimed a higher attention than any other object of worship. People are, however, buried with their faces towards the rising sun. The belief that the sun dances at his rising on Easter Sunday may be found in several collections of English folk-lore as well as here. Some have attempted to explain this belief by pretending that the popular notion is that the sun dances for joy because of the resurrection of Christ from the dead. The belief may be connected with the worship of Éastre, the dawn-goddess, but it has certainly not arisen from the Christian Resurrection. The man who gets up early on Easter morning to see the sun dance cannot tell why he does so. But his forefathers may have believed that the sun dances for joy at the resurrection of Spring from her wintry tomb. Christian festivals, like pagan, follow the course of the seasons. Christ, at the season of Yule tide, represents the birth of the year, and his rising from the dead is celebrated upon the return of spring. The old feasts are kept, and the old rites are followed, under new names, and even the name may remain, as it does in Easter. Though we may not find any actual survival of sun-worship, there are many survivals in England of the use of a well-known sun symbol. The sign of the cross, as found in the following pages, does not derive its origin from the instrument of the passion of Jesus. The laying of two straws across each other to make the rain cease, the making of this sign on the hand when a solitary crow crosses one's path, or on water in which another person has washed, the crossing of wort in the brewing vat to "keep out the witch," the fixing of a cross behind one's bedroom door to keep evil spirits away, the stitching of a twig into the dress in the form of a cross, the carrying about upon the person of a cross of "witch-wiggin" as a protection against witchcraft, the "putting out" of a rain-bow by laying two twigs or straws across each other—these and similar practices are neither borrowed nor derived from the cross of Calvary. In China a mother dips her finger in the ashes of dried banana-skin and paints a cross on the forehead of her sleeping babe "to avert the calamity of nursing a demon." * In our English churches the priest dips his finger in the water of the font and crosses the child's forehead, and we shall see hereafter that mothers in Derbyshire take a plate of salt into church at baptism, showing that in former times salt and water, like the ashes of the banana-skin, were regarded in

* *F. L. Journal*, quoted by Mr. Hartland in *The Science of Fairy Tales*, p. 97.

England as a protection against evil spirits and changelings. In all these cases the cross was the " wheel cross " or " ring cross," the sign for the sun-god, which may be seen figured on many heathen remains of northern Europe, and particularly on the famous bronze trumpet or horn found at Wismar in Mecklenburg.* We may ask ourselves, How did people begin to entertain the notion that the crossing of two straws would cause the rain to cease or the rainbow to go out? To answer this question we must try to bring ourselves down to the mental state of uncivilised or savage races who knew nothing of natural laws, and who attempted to account for natural phenomena in a way which seemed right to them. A savage would not fail to observe that the rain ceases when the sun shines brightly, and he would, in his way of reasoning, regard the sun as a being or power which, amongst other powers, had the power to make the rain cease. He would also consider that similar appearances produce similar effects, and therefore he would consider that if the sun can make the rain cease and the rainbow vanish, an image made in the likeness of the sun might have the same effect. Now the sun was regarded as a chariot drawn by horses, and hence the primitive man would make use of the sun-sign—the spokes of the sun-wheel—by laying two straws across or otherwise making the sign of the cross. The churches and churchyards of England still contain old stone monuments whereon the sun-wheel is carved, either as a separate emblem standing by the side of the Christian cross, or as forming part of or interwoven with the Christian cross. And so the cross on the tomb, like the cross on the child's forehead made as a protection against evil, would, in savage reasoning, protect the body beneath from the powers of darkness. Again, the cocks on our church steeples seem to have been originally placed there in the hope that they would induce fine weather. I have recorded the belief that " if a cock crows on a high building the weather will be fine."† Early reasoning may have taken this form: when

---

* Worsaae's *Industrial Arts of Denmark*, 1882, p. 66.

† *Post*, p. 66. Compare the " cock-crowing stones " mentioned on a subsequent page.

cocks crow on a high place it will be fine ; therefore, if we put a cock (or image of a cock) on the church steeple we shall attract fine weather. Our ancestors associated light and dawn with cock-crowing, and, in their barbarous reasoning, believed that cock-crowing brought the day.

A similar method of reasoning might be shown in a hundred examples, and a considerable number of such examples is given in the following pages. Amongst them may be mentioned the belief that a man can be tortured by injuring an image made to resemble him, or the belief that warts can be removed by burying green peas in the ground in the expectation that as the peas decay the warts will decay also, or in burning an effigy, or in sticking pins into the body of a live frog, or into the heart of a pigeon, for the purpose of causing pain or even death to an inconstant lover or to an enemy.

Consciously or unconsciously, those who made the sign of the cross were attempting, by the magical influence of a rude image of the sun, as seen in the spokes of the " sun-wheel " ($\oplus$), to do things which, in primitive or savage belief, the sun has the power to do, as, for instance, to make the rain cease.

We may follow this strange reasoning to the seasons of the year, and we may expect à priori that a similar kind of reasoning would be applied to the calendar. And we have the clearest evidence that it was so. Before we consider the evidence let me first of all give an illustration of the method of reasoning employed. In one of Mr. Du Maurier's drawings in Punch a child is represented as wagging a big dog's tail to make the dog happy. It is quite possible that a child might reason from his own observation in this way : dogs are happy when they wag their tails ; therefore if I wag a dog's tail I shall make him happy. And, as we have already seen, it is certain that primitive man did reason in this way. So when a Derbyshire man puts a coin into the spout on New Year's Eve and brings it into the house the minute after the clock has struck twelve at midnight, what is his object in so doing? Clearly to make the coming year prosperous. Just as the child in Punch wags the dog's tail to make him happy, so the Derbyshire man brings a coin into the house to make the new year prosperous. It may be that when he does this he is quite unconscious of what the ceremony means, and that he is merely repeating a formality whose meaning has long been forgotten. Still there once was a time when his ancestors practised the ceremony with a real and earnest purpose. A similar rude process of reasoning goes on, or at least once went on, when a piece of money is put into the pocket of a new coat "for luck," the idea being that the coin will have a magical influence over the coat, and that the pro·sperity thus begun will be continued. A year or two ago a great disturbance arose amongst the cattle-drovers and butchers of Nottinghamshire about what they called "luck money." It seems that when a butcher bought a cow or other animal it was customary for the cattle-drover to return a small portion of the purchase money "for luck," and this custom the cattle-drovers sought to break down on the ground that it was an unfair tax on them. The matter was agitated with great vehemence, and many stormy meetings were held. But everybody had forgotten what the "luck money" really meant. To one portion of these agitators it seemed but a mere tax or unfair imposition, though it once had a serious and real significance, for the giving of a coin to the purchaser was intended to bring good luck to him or to the purchased animal itself, just as the taking of a coin into the house on New Year's Eve, or the putting of a coin into the pocket of a new coat, was intended to bring good luck to the house and coat respectively. Arising in the beginning from rude and erroneous notions of cause and effect, this "luck money" came to be regarded as a magical means of inducing good fortune, and finally as an unfair tax which ought to be removed by organised resistance.

To return to the calendar, from which we have digressed, we have seen that the bringing of a coin into the house at the dawn of the New Year was believed to be a means of ensuring the possession of money during that year. But important as it was that the household should be possessed of money, it was more important that it should have enough of food and fire. It was therefore desirable that as the year came in some means

should be devised whereby the possession of these good things
would be secured. Now as regards food, it happens that
amongst the superstitious beliefs recorded in this collection is
one which declares that "if you refuse a mince pie at Christmas you will be unlucky during the following year." We learn
therefore that the partaking of a mixed dish or cake as the new
year comes in was believed to induce a sufficiency of food, and
thus our Christmas mince pie must be regarded in the light of a
charm or instrument of magic. The very number of ingredients
of which mince pie is made, such as meat, fruit, flour, and so
forth, shows its original purpose, all these things being regarded
as necessities of life.

It will be seen on a subsequent page that in Derbyshire a
species of cake called "wassil cake," compounded in the same
way as another cake well known in magic as "the speechless
cake," is made on New Year's Day. Though we cannot be
certain that our Christmas mince pie is a degenerate form of
the "wassil cake," we are at least sure that it was believed to
induce "luck," or a sufficiency of food, and it would be strange
if the older "wassil cake," so wonderfully compounded, were
not intended for the same purpose. There is nothing in the
present collection more interesting than the too brief description
of the Christmas feast once held in the farmhouses of South
Yorkshire. Though we may smile at its rudeness, that simple feast
at Penistone * has all the solemnity of a sacred rite. It shows
us the house-father and his family sitting round their table at
the hour when, according to ancient belief, the spirits of dead
men so filled the air that men feared to be alone, and partaking
each in his turn of the food and drink which were to bless the
coming year by a sufficiency of those good things.

Just as the Christmas cake and the piece of money were
intended as harbingers of food and wealth, so the Yule log and
the big Christmas candle were intended to have a magic influence
in securing warmth and light during the coming year. And
can it not be said that the sprigs of evergreen brought into the

* P. 103.

house at the dawn of the opening year were intended as harbingers of good crops and plenteous harvests? The origin of the festival customs which usher in Christmas or the New Year must not be sought in the desire to express joy at the birth of a Saviour, or even to express joy at the birth of the New Year. We must look for that origin in the magical effect which the presence of food, warmth, light, and money in the house on New Year's morning was supposed to have upon the year which was to come.

But how can we explain the dark-haired "lucky bird," or the dark-haired man or boy who must be the first to enter the house on Christmas morning? It is just possible that we may find the explanation in the fact that the aboriginal and conquered race which once occupied these islands was dark-skinned and black-haired. If it be objected that such an inference would be vitiated by the fact that the incomer must always be of the male sex, and that we have therefore a mixed magical omen, the answer is that a woman must not enter the house on Christmas Day at all,* probably because she, being "the weaker vessel," would bring weakness and not strength into the household. But, of course, a contrary belief that the man must be light-haired, as recorded by Mr. Henderson, would, if the belief were at all general, be a fatal objection to this supposition.† However, Mr. Henderson has told us that in the north of England the first person to enter the house must have "a high-arched instep, a foot that 'water runs under.'"‡ With regard to the high instep, Dr. Tylor of Oxford tells me that his impression is that it is the Spaniards who pride themselves on it, and I have heard this from other sources. The old Northern poem Rigsmál, believed by its editors to have been written by a Dane living in the British Isles about the eleventh century, describes the thrall as of swarthy skin, as having long heels, and a snub nose (nidr-biúgt nef), that is a short or stumpy nose with the end cut off § The negro is said to have long heels,

* P. 106, *post.*
† *Folk-lore of the Northern Counties,* 1879, p. 73; and see *post,* p. 106.
‡ Henderson, p. 74.
§ *Corpus Poet. Boreale,* i. 236, 515.

but in a letter to me Dr. Tylor says, " I once looked into the alleged peculiarity of the negro as to projecting heel, but did not find it well borne out by facts, and should not assert it with·out a good deal more proof than I have seen." In discussing the question of the secluded Lincolnshire " Yellow Bellies," Dr. Morton of Sheffield, who was born in a Lincolnshire village, tells me that he never thought that the Yellow Bellies " were of the colour we now call yellow, but something of a bronze shade, and never, I believe, in company with light hair and eyes." And he says, " In Alford, my native town, there is a part occupied by a set who have a bad name, and with whom the ordinary farm labourer will have nothing to do. They are poachers, hawkers, and tinkers, rarely regular labourers, and they are sometimes ignorantly supposed to be gypsies." It is interesting to observe that in Wyclif's translation of the Bible, yellow translates *furvus* in the Vulgate, *i.e.*, dusky, swarthy. And then we must remember that the gypsies are feared, and that the people believe in their magical powers.* If more evidence of this kind could be got together it might be inferred that the dark-haired " lucky bird " or " first foot " who must " let in " Christmas was originally a member of a dark-skinned subject race, and a very important conclusion might also be drawn as to the nationality of the long-heeled, snub-nosed thrall in Rigsmál. And let us not forget the well-known tendency of conquering races to ascribe magical powers to the conquered.

In the chapter recording " Local and Ceremonial Customs " it is said that a woman must bind at least one sheaf at harvest, and that she must also assist in the planting of seeds, such as potatoes, the belief being that a crop will not flourish unless a woman has had a hand either in the sowing or the harvesting. It seems most reasonable to explain this custom, or rather the belief which gave rise to the custom, by reference to a savage process of reasoning which may be formulated thus : women are fertile, for they bring forth children ; therefore a crop will be fertile if a woman take part in the sowing. By an analogous

* *Post*, pp. 93, 94.

process of barbarous reasoning the whole course of the crop, from sowing to harvesting, would be rendered more prosperous by association with a woman. The belief may, however, be a survival from a time when women cultivated the soil, as modern Africans do now.

One of the most interesting relics of paganism which I have had the good luck to discover is that which relates to the three Fates or Norns. In the section entitled "Two Pagan Hymns" mention will be found of three maids known as "the threble Thribers," two of whom are "lily white," and the third is dressed in green. These maids are described as living for evermore, and they are plainly the three Fates. The same beings are also twice mentioned elsewhere in this collection. The girls who set the table on New Year's Eve with knives, forks, plates, and chairs for three guests, whom they expect to appear at the hour of midnight, are, without knowing it, spreading the table for the three Fates, though in the charm which they practise they expect their future husbands to appear.* In the collection of superstitions condemned by Burchard, Bishop of Worms, who died in 1024, we are told that the German women of his time had the custom, at certain times of the year, of spreading tables in their houses with meat and drink, and laying three knives, that if the three sisters should come (whom Burchard interprets as being equivalent to the Roman Parcae) they might partake of their hospitality.† Thus, in a Derbyshire village, at the end of the nineteenth century, we find this old superstition in full vigour, the only difference being that the future husbands of the women, instead of the Fates, are expected to appear. In the Nornagests Saga we are told that there travelled about in the land *völvur*, who are called *spákonur*, who foretold to men their fate. People invited them to their houses and gave

---

* P. 84.

† Wright's *Celt, Roman, and Saxon*, 4th ed., p. 340. Burchard's words are : "Fecisti ut quaedam mulieres in quibusdam temporibus anni facere solent, ut in domo sua mensam praeparares et tuos cibos et potum cum tribus cultellis supra mensam poneres, ut si venissent tres illae sorores, quas antiqua posteritas et antiqua stultitia Parcas nominavit, ibi reficerentur."

them good cheer and gifts. These beings are identical with the Norns.*

A very striking account was given to me of the appearance of the Fates on the common at Cold-Aston, in the parish of Dronfield. The narrator spoke of "three tall, thin women standing in a line with three hour glasses in their hands," of "a tall man three yards high with an oak tree over his shoulder," and of "a man with a scythe over his shoulder." He said that "the appearance of the women with the hour glasses meant that such or such a person had not more than three hours to live," that the giant with the oak tree came to tell that person's age, the tree being a young tree if the person were young, and an old tree if he were old. The man with the scythe came to cut the person down. The "three tall, thin women standing in a line" are the Norns, and if I had found an old marble statue of the *Matres Deae* buried on the common I could not have been more astonished than I was when I heard these words. This popular remembrance, handed down in England through so many ages, of the awful divinities

$$\text{άίτε βροτοῖσιν}$$
$$\text{γεινομένοισι διδοῦσιν ἔχειν ἀγαθόν τε κακόν τε}$$

was too plain to be misunderstood.

The existence of divinities implies sacrifice, and we shall see that sacrifice to pagan divinities still continues in England. In some collieries in North Derbyshire the colliers leave in the pit every week a hundredweight of coal " for the fairies." When children gather fruit, such as blackberries or bilberries, in the woods or on the moors, they throw the first fruit which they have plucked behind their backs and say, " Pray God send me good luck to-day." Here we have distinct offerings of first-fruits to the local deities—*diis campestribus*. Another offering of first-fruits may be seen in the practice of setting *two* beans, or seeds of any kind, at the beginning of a row which is planted singly, and in the throwing up of a spade full of earth when

---

* Grimm's *Teut. Myth.*, trans. by Stallybrass, p. 409.

one hires or buys a piece of land, in the belief that the crops will not prosper unless these things are done. And then we have the custom, till lately prevalent in the High Peak, of dropping pins into wells as votive offerings to the "fairies" or goddesses who presided over them.

The sacred character of salt comes out very clearly in our collection. A mixture of salt and water, called "holy lymph," will purify a dead man's garment. Prayers offered near to salt will be answered. Oaths are taken on salt, and a child which is baptized near a plate of salt brought by the parents into church will be sure to go to heaven.

We shall meet with the strange fancy that the souls of the dead dwell in flowers. I have recorded the belief that souls dwell in the flowers of the broad bean (*faba vulgaris*), and that the hawthorn has "a deathly smell." We are also told that the fairies, which are the souls of the dead, dwell in foxglove bells, and the reader will be reminded of Ariel's song in the *Tempest*:

> Where the bee sucks, there suck I:
> In a cowslip's bell I lie.

The belief that accidents are frequent when broad beans are in flower means that the presence of unhallowed spirits in those flowers is fraught with harm to the neighbourhood. Connected with this belief is the association of murdered men's ghosts with a sweet odour of thyme. The more luscious or sweet-smelling flowers appear to have been their favourite abodes; the sweeter the perfume, the more dangerous the ghost. The English fairy tale of Jack and the Bean Stalk may be connected with the belief that souls dwell in bean flowers.

The custom of preserving lost teeth in a jar till burial is practised in South Yorkshire, and in the northern parts of Derbyshire. It is related to the old practice of burying the dead with their clothes, weapons, shoes, and even food, in their tombs—a practice which arose from the well-known belief, current amongst uncivilised men, that the dead require the bodily equipments which they have had in life.

The inhuman practice of burying children alive in the foundations of buildings, as a sacrifice to the local deity to ensure the stability of such buildings, seems to come out in the nursery rime printed on p. 147. In it the nurse is telling how a man had a child, how he put the child into various things, such as a log of wood, an apple pasty, and other impossible situations, until at last she comes to the climax, and says:

> He put him in an old house side,
> And there he lived, and there he died,
> And nobody either laughed or cried.

She is telling what happened in the old days. They walled the child up alive in the foundation, where it lived a few hours or a few days and died.* And as this was a sacrifice or religious duty "nobody either laughed or cried."

I have recorded the popular belief that Morris dancing is fairy dancing, that Morris dancing means fairy dancing, and that the dance itself was "taken away from the fairies." There are some people who attribute nearly everything for which they cannot account to the fairies. Still the belief is remarkable, and not without significance. It implies the further belief that the fairies, or dead men's ghosts, once danced on the Derbyshire hills, and makes us understand the lines:

> The piper of Shacklow,
> The fiddler of Finn ;
> The old woman of Demon's Dale
> Calls them all in.

There is something beautiful and strange in the music to which the Morris dancers dance.† If ever music were not of this world it was this. To hear it is to believe that Morris dancing was a religious rite. Has it not descended to us from a dusky Iberian people, once a distinct caste in England,

---

* See the chapter on "Foundation Sacrifice" in my *Hall of Wathcof*, 1893, p. 62.

† Printed on p. 136 by the kindness of T. W. Froggatt, Esq., formerly of Eyam.

c

in whose magical powers and religion the dominant races believed?

In his Dictionary Professor Skeat has concluded that a Morris dancer was a Moorish dancer. Assuming that such is the case, we may ask ourselves why these dancers were so called. Are we to suppose that English peasants borrowed the dance from the Moors in historical times? Or are we to believe that it was handed down in England from an early period by the remnants of a dark-coloured Iberian people who, according to Tacitus, crossed over from Spain,* and were, in fact, Moors? In Yorkshire a rude Christmas play, known as "The Peace Egg," is performed. In that play the chief act is the slaughter by St. George of England of a "Black Prince of Paradine," whom St. George stigmatizes as a "black Morocco dog." The play seems to represent an old feud between a light-haired and a dark-haired people once inhabiting England; and it may be that in the popular speech the dark-haired people were once known here as Moors. If this dramatized contest between St. George of England and the "black Morocco dog" does not point back to a time when conflicts existed in this country between a dusky race of Iberian or Moorish origin and a light-haired people which conquered and enslaved them, to what can we ascribe its origin? We can only say that the play is of historical or literary, and not of traditional, origin. But the form of the play renders an historical or literary origin impossible, and the whole performance seems to be nothing else but a rude and popular reminiscence of an ancient national feud. And I would draw attention to the fact that Morris is an ancient surname in England.

It seems relevant to mention here an old earthwork, extending for some miles in length, near Sheffield, known in one part of its course as Barber Balk.† The direction of the earthwork is from south-west to north-east, and the ditch is uniformly on the southern side, as if it had been intended as a defence against

---

* *Agricola*, 11.

† See my *Hall of Walthcof*, pp. 22, 242, *seq.*, where other instances of place-names beginning with "Barber" are given.

attack delivered from that side. Some modern scholars identify the Barbars, or Berbers, a people inhabiting Barbary, or the Saracen countries along the north coast of Africa, with the Iberians.* Can it be that an invading Celtic people threw up this earthwork as a defence against a dusky Iberian foe coming from the south, and that the ancient name of the earth-work has been handed down from a remote time, thereby pre-serving its true history? And is it not possible that the Iberian, the Morris or Moor, the "black Morocco dog" of the traditional play, and the Barber are identical? A great authority on early Britain "has accepted and employed the theory advanced by ethnologists that the early inhabitants of this country were of Iberian origin."† This earthwork was known in one part of its course as Danes Balk, and is known in another part as Barber Balk. Is it unreasonable to suppose that the "Dane" was a Cimbrian invader coming from the Cimbric or Danish penin-sula, and that the "Barber" was his Iberian enemy? In determining the age of any prehistoric earthwork, excavation is, of course, desirable, and as regards the earthwork here mentioned this remains to be done. The discovery, however, of flint implements and Roman coins upon and in the mounds points to a very early origin.

With a view to a further and enlarged edition of this book, I should be thankful for other stories of the kind here printed, and for old traditions and folk-lore. Contributions, which will be duly acknowledged, should be sent to me at 3, Westbourne Road, Sheffield.

My thanks are hereby tendered to those who have put into my hands the material here printed. Amongst these I must particularly mention Mrs. Turner of Leeds, and formerly of Norton, in Derbyshire, Mr. T. W. Froggatt, Mr. F. J. Smith, Mr. R. F. Drury, the Rev. W. Slater Sykes, the late Mr. William Furness, Mrs. Hutton. Miss Alice Halifax has obtained a very large portion both of the tales and traditional

* See an article on the Iberians in *Encyclop. Brit.*
† Prof. Rhys in *Celtic Britain*, p. vii.

remains from informants whose lips would have revealed little to me, and I am indebted to Mrs. Hugh Tomasson, of Broomhill, Sheffield, for many curious items of folk-lore, obtained chiefly from the East Riding.

Originally I intended to include in this book a collection of games which I had made. But as Mrs. Gomme was printing her *Traditional Games*, I gave them to her, and they are now being printed in that excellent work.

In these days the value of tradition is not likely to be called in question, nor is it so easily falsified as the inexperienced may think. Like the common law, or *lex non scripta*, it abides in the memories of the people, and they, in varying degrees of fidelity, have handed it down from age to age.

HOUSEHOLD TALES.

1.—THE SMALL-TOOTH DOG.*

ONCE upon a time there was a merchant who travelled about the world a great deal. On one of his journeys thieves attacked him, and they would have taken both his life and his money if a large dog had not come to his rescue and driven the thieves away.

When the dog had driven the thieves away he took the merchant to his house, which was a very handsome one, and he dressed his wounds and nursed him until he was well.

As soon as he was able to travel the merchant began his journey home, but before starting he told the dog how grateful he was for his kindness, and asked him what reward he could offer in return, and he said he would not refuse to give him the most precious thing that he had.

And so the merchant said to the dog, " Will you accept a fish that I have that can speak twelve languages ? "

" No," said the dog, " I will not."

" Or a goose that lays golden eggs ? "

" No," said the dog, " I will not."

" Or a mirror in which you can see what anybody is thinking about ? "

" No," said the dog, " I will not."

* From Norton, in Derbyshire.

B

"Then what will you have?" said the merchant.

"I will have none of such presents," said the dog, "but let me fetch your daughter and take her to my house."

When the merchant heard this he was grieved, but what he had promised had to be done, so he said to the dog, "You can come and fetch my daughter after I have been at home for a week."

So at the end of the week the dog came to the merchant's house to fetch his daughter, but when he got there he stayed outside the door, and would not go in.

But the merchant's daughter did as her father told her, and came out of the house dressed for a journey and ready to go with the dog.

When the dog saw her he looked pleased, and said: "Jump on my back, and I will take you away to my house."

So she mounted on the dog's back, and away they went at a great pace until they reached the dog's house, which was many miles off.

But after she had been a month at the dog's house she began to mope and cry.

"What are you crying for?" said the dog.

"Because I want to go back to my father," she said.

The dog said, "If you will promise me that you will not stay at home more than three days I will take you there. But, first of all," said he, "what do you call me?"

"A great, foul, small-tooth dog," said she.

"Then," said he, "I will not let you go."

But she cried so pitifully that he promised again to take her home. "But before we start," said he, "tell me what you call me."

"Oh," she said, "your name is Sweet-as-a-honeycomb."

"Jump on my back," said he, "and I'll take you home."

So he trotted away with her on his back for forty miles, when they came to a stile.

"And what do you call me?" said he, before they got over the stile.

Thinking that she was safe on her way, the girl said, "A great, foul, small-tooth dog."

But when she said this he did not jump over the stile, but turned right round about at once, and galloped back to his own house with the girl on his back.

Another week went by, and again the girl wept so bitterly that the dog promised her again to take her to her father's house.

So the girl got on the dog's back again, and they reached the first stile as before, and then the dog stopped and said, "And what do you call me?"

"Sweet-as-a-honeycomb," she replied.

So the dog leaped over the stile, and they went on for twenty miles until they came to another stile.

"And what do you call me?" said the dog, with a wag of his tail.

She was thinking more of her father and her own home than of the dog, so she answered, "A great, foul, small-tooth dog."

Then the dog was in a great rage, and he turned right round about and galloped back to his own house as before.

After she had cried for another week the dog promised again to take her back to her father's house. So she mounted upon his back once more, and when they got to the first stile the dog said, "And what do you call me?"

"Sweet-as-a-honeycomb," she said.

So the dog jumped over the stile, and away they went— for now the girl made up her mind to say the most loving things she could think of—until they reached her father's house.

When they got to the door of the merchant's house the dog said, "And what do you call me?"

Just at that moment the girl forgot the loving things that she meant to say, and began, "A great——" but the dog began to turn, and she got fast hold of the door latch, and was going to say "foul," when she saw how grieved the dog looked and remembered how good and patient he had been with her, so she said, " Sweeter-than-a-honeycomb."

When she had said this she thought the dog would have been content and have galloped away, but instead of that he suddenly stood up on his hind legs, and with his fore legs he pulled off his dog's head and tossed it high in the air. His hairy coat dropped off, and there stood the handsomest young man in the world, with the finest and smallest teeth you ever saw.

Of course they were married, and lived together happily.

2.—THE BAG OF NUTS.*

It happened once that two young men met in a churchyard, about eight o'clock in the evening.

One of them said to the other, " Where are you going ? "

The other answered, " I'm going to get a bag of nuts that lies underneath my mother's head in this churchyard. But tell me, where are you going ? "

He said, " I'm going to steal a fat sheep out of this field. Wait here till I come back."

Then the other man got the nuts that were under his dead mother's head, and stood in the church porch cracking them. In those days it was the custom to ring a bell at a certain time in the evening, and just as the man was cracking the nuts the sexton came into the churchyard to ring it. But when he heard the cracking of the nuts in the porch he was afraid, and ran to tell the parson, who only laughed at him, and said, " Go and ring, fool." However, the sexton was so afraid, that he said he would not go back unless the parson would go with him. After much persuasion the parson agreed to go, but he had the gout very badly, and the sexton

---

* From Calver, in Derbyshire. Another version of this story is given in *A Hundred Mery Talys*, 1526, reprinted by Oesterley in 1866.

had to carry him on his back. When the man in the porch who was cracking the nuts saw the sexton coming into the churchyard with the parson on his back he thought it was the man who had just gone out to steal the sheep, and had returned with a sheep on his back. So he bawled out, " Is it a fat one ? " * When the sexton heard this he was so frightened that he threw the parson down and said, " Aye, and thou canst take it if thou lik'st." So the sexton ran away as fast as he could, and left the parson to shift for himself. But the parson ran home as fast as the sexton.

3.—THE TAILOR AND HIS APPRENTICES.†

THERE was once a country tailor who had two apprentices, and he used to keep them at work till eleven o'clock at night. One day the tailor had to go to the town to buy cloth, and he came back late in the evening, passing on his way home through a lonely wood. The apprentices, who knew that he would come home through the wood, went out after dark, and got up a tree near the footpath on which they knew that their master would pass. In a short time they heard the tailor coming, and one of them called out " Abraham." The tailor answered, " Yes, my Lord," thinking it was God who had spoken to him. One of the apprentices in the tree said :

> If thou keepest thy lads at work till eleven
> Thou shalt not enter the kingdom of heaven.

When the tailor had gone the boys ran quickly home by a shorter way, and were at work when their master reached the house. As soon as he had opened the door he said to them, " Put your work away, lads, put your work away," and they were never kept so late at work afterwards.

---

* " Estne bene pinguis quem portas?" So in a version of the story quoted by Oesterley from the *Scala Celi*, 1480.
† From Calver, in Derbyshire.

4.—THE BOY WHO FEARED NOTHING.*

ONCE a father made a bet with his son that he dare not go into the bone-house in their village churchyard at midnight and fetch a skull out without taking a light with him.

The son accepted the wager, and on the following night went down into the bone-house.

In the meantime the father had told a man to hide himself in the bone-house, and watch the boy.

When the boy got down amongst the bones, he picked up a skull. Then the man who had hidden himself said, "Don't take that, for that's my mother's skull." So the boy threw it down, and picked up another skull, when the man said, "Don't take that, for that's my grandmother's." So the boy threw that down, and picked another up, but the man said, "And that's my grandfather's." Then the boy shouted, "Why, they're all thy mother's, or thy grandmother's; but I've come for a skull, and I'll have one." So the boy picked one up and ran home to his father, and won the wager.

5.—THE ENCHANTED MOUNTAIN.†

ONE Sunday afternoon, as two children, named Kate and Willie, came out of church, they agreed to go for a walk together. So they walked on until they came to a large mountain, which made everyone who went near it go to sleep. As they drew near to the mountain they began to be sleepy, and at last they both fell asleep at the foot of the mountain. After they had lain there awhile a giant came

* From Calver, in Derbyshire. Compare Grimm, No. 4. In the notes Grimm mentions a similar story from the neighbourhood of Paderhorn, in which a bone-house is mentioned.

† From North Derbyshire. The league boots denote the swift pace of the giant. Grimm's *Teut. Myth.*, p. 1443.

by, and woke the children up, saying that he would take the boy and kill him, and keep Kate to clean his four-and-twenty league boots. So he took them to his castle, which was on the top of the mountain, and gave them in charge of the old woman who kept house for him. Willie soon escaped from the castle, but Kate could not find her way out. When the giant arose the next morning and found the boy gone he was very angry, and the first thing that he did was to make Kate clean his boots. After the boots were cleaned he said, " I will go and bathe me in the river, and thou, Kate, shalt go with me, and hold in thy hands this golden ring and golden ball." Now Kate knew that if you put the ball inside the ring and wished something your wish would be granted. When the giant had got well into the water, Kate slipped the ball into the ring, and wished that the giant were leagues away and herself safe in her own village. Immediately she found herself walking up the village street, and meeting her father and mother and Willie coming out to seek her. And so Kate became the owner of the ring and the ball, and whenever after that she wished anything her wish was granted.

6.—JACK THE BUTTER-MILK.*

JACK was a boy who sold butter-milk. One day as he was going his rounds he met a witch who asked him for some of his butter-milk, and told him that if he refused to give it she would put him into a bag that she carried over her shoulders.

But Jack would not give the witch any of his butter-milk, so she put him into her bag, and walked off home with him.

But as she was going on her way she suddenly remembered that she had forgotten a pot of fat that she had

---

* Such was the title of the story given to me. It comes from Nottingham-shire.

bought in the town. Now Jack was too heavy to be carried back to the town, so the witch asked some men who were brushing the hedge by the roadside if they would take care of her bag until she came back.

The men promised to take care of the bag, but when the witch had gone Jack called out to them and said, "If you will take me out of this bag and fill it full of thorns I will give you some of my butter-milk."

So the men took Jack out of the bag and filled it with thorns, and then Jack gave them some butter-milk, and ran home.

When the witch came back from the town she picked up her bag, threw it over her shoulder, and walked away. But she had not gone far before the thorns began to prick her back, and she said, "Jack, I think thou'st got some pins about thee, lad."

As soon as she had got home she emptied the bag upon a clean white sheet that she had ready. But when she found that there was nothing in the bag but thorns she was very angry and said, "I'll catch thee to-morrow, Jack, and I'll boil thee."

The next day she met Jack again, and asked him for some butter-milk, and told him that if he would not give it her she would put him into her bag again. But Jack said he would give her no butter-milk, so she put him into her bag, and again she bethought her that she had forgotten something for which she would have to go back to the town.

This time she left the bag with some men who were mending the road. Now as soon as the witch had gone Jack called out to them and said, "If you will take me out and fill this bag full of stones I will give you some of my butter-milk."

Then the men took Jack out of the bag, and he gave them the butter-milk.

When the witch came back she threw the bag over her shoulder as before, and when she heard the stones grinding and rattling she chuckled and said, "My word, Jack, thy bones do crack."

When she got home she emptied the bag on the white sheet again. But when she saw the stones she was very angry, and swore that she would boil Jack when she caught him.

The next day she went out as before, and met Jack again, and asked for some butter-milk. But Jack said, "No," again, so she put him into her bag, and went straight home with him, and threw him out upon the white sheet.

When she had done this she went out of the house and locked Jack in, intending to boil him when she came back. But whilst she was away Jack opened all the cupboards in the house and filled the bag with all the pots that he could find. After he had done this he escaped through the chimney, and got safe home.

When the witch came back she emptied the bag upon the sheet again, and broke all the pots that she had in the house. After this she never caught Jack any more.

7.—DATHERA DAD.*

THERE was once a farmer's wife who made a pudding and set it on the fire to be boiled. As soon as the water began to boil the pudding jumped, and at last it jumped out upon the floor and rolled about as if it were bewitched. As the pudding was rolling about on the floor a travelling tinker came to the door, and the woman picked the pudding up and gave it to him. So the tinker put it into his budget and slung it over his back. As he trudged along the road the pudding kept rolling about in the budget till at last it broke in pieces, when out came a little fairy child who cried : "Take me to my dathera dad, take me to my dathera dad."

* From Eyam, in Derbyshire. Compare the preceding tale and compare both stories with " Johnny-Cake " (No. xxviii.) in Mr. Jacobs' *English Fairy Tales*. David Nutt, 1890. Is " dathera " related to Icel. daðra, to wheedle ?

8.—JACK OTTER.*

IN Lincolnshire there once lived a man, called Jack Otter, who had been married nine times, and had murdered all his wives one after another. One day he was angry with the woman that he was courting, and whom he intended to take for his tenth wife. So he asked her to go for a walk with him, and when they had got into a lonely place he stabbed her and buried her on the spot. But his crime was found out, and he was gibbeted on a post in the lane. Now a bird, called the willow-biter, built her nest in the dead man's mouth as he hung on the gallows tree, and brought up her fledgelings in it. And hence this riddle is asked:

There were ten tongues within one head ;
And one went out to fetch some bread
To feed the living in the dead.

9.—THE GIRL WHO GOT UP THE TREE.†

A GIRL who was leaving her master's service at a farm in the country told her sweetheart that she would meet him near a stile where they had met many times before. This stile was overhung by a tree. The girl got there before him and found a hole dug underneath the tree, and a pickaxe and spade lying by the side of the hole. She was much frightened at what she saw, and got up the tree. After she had been up the tree awhile her sweetheart came, and

* From Lincolnshire. Compare the next story. Otter here stands for Höttr, the hatted one, a name of Odin, on account of the slouching hat or hood which he wore. In Hava-mal Odin says, "I mind me hanging on the gallows-tree nine whole nights, wounded with the spear, offered to Odin, myself to myself ; on the tree, whose roots no man knoweth. They gave me no loaf ; they held no horn to me." Vigfusson and Powell's *Corpus Poeticum Boreale*, i. p. 24.

† From North Derbyshire. Compare the preceding tale, and a tale in Halliwell's *Popular Rhymes and Nursery Tales*, 1849 p. 49 called " The Oxford Student."

another man with him. Thinking that the girl had not yet come, the two men began to talk, and the girl heard her sweetheart say, "She will not come to-night. We'll go home now, and come back and kill her to-morrow night." As soon as they had gone the girl came down the tree and ran home to her father. When she had told him what she had seen, the father pondered awhile and then said to his daughter: "We will have a feast and ask our friends, and we will ask thy sweetheart to come and the man that came with him to the tree." So the two men came along with the other guests. In the evening they began to ask riddles of each other, but the girl who had got up the tree was the last to ask hers. She said :

> I'll rede you a riddle, I'll rede it you right,
> Where was I last Saturday night ?
> The wind did blow, the leaves did shake,
> When I saw the hole the fox did make.*

When the two men who had intended to murder the girl heard this they ran out of the house.

10.—THE LITTLE WATERCRESS GIRL.†

THERE was once a little girl who had to sell watercresses for her living because she was very poor. One day she met an old witch who said to her, "If you will come and help me to keep my house I will sell your watercresses for you."

The little girl said, "I will try my best."

"But there is one thing you must promise me," said the witch, "and that is this : you must not look up the chimney."

* The following variation occurs :
> One moonlight night as I sat high
> Waiting for one but two came by,
> The boughs did bend, my heart did quake
> To see the hole the fox did make.

† From Nottinghamshire.

The girl promised that she would not, and went to live at the witch's house. After she had been there a few days she wanted badly to look up the chimney, and she said to herself, "Surely there would be no harm in just having one peep."

So she peeped up the chimney, and saw a white bag there, and pulled it down. Then she opened it and found that it was full of money. Her eyes glistened at the sight of so much wealth, and she said, "I mean to keep this, for I am very poor."

So she carried the bag of money into an orchard close by where many fruit-trees grew.

First of all she went up to the apple-tree, and said, "Apple-tree, apple-tree, hide me; and if any one shall ask thee whether thou hast seen me, say 'I have not.'"

So the apple-tree promised to hide her. When the witch came back and found that her bag of money was gone she looked everywhere for the little watercress girl. She searched all through the house, and at last she went into the orchard.

First of all she went up to the gooseberry-bush, and said, "Gooseberry-bush, gooseberry-bush, hast thou seen a little girl with a white bag in her hand?"

But the gooseberry-bush said, "Nay." Then the witch went to every tree in the garden, asking each the same question, but all the trees said, "Nay."

At last she came to the apple-tree, which said "Nay," like the other trees.

So the little girl was hidden by the apple-tree, and when the witch had gone to bed she carried the bag of money home.

11.—THE HAWK AND THE PARROT.*

ONE day as a parrot was walking about in a garden a hawk came and flew away with her. As the hawk was carrying

* From Calver, in Derbyshire.

the parrot over a field the parrot saw a ploughman who had weak, sore knees, and called out to him, " I say, old rotten shins, I ride, I ride ! "

The ploughman answered, " Aye, and thou'lt have to pay for it soon."

The hawk then flew into the hedge on the other side of the field and began to pluck the parrot's feathers off. Whilst he was doing this the parrot kept crying, " Oh, damn thee, thou lugs, thou lugs ! "

After a struggle the parrot got loose and went and told the ploughman how the hawk had lugged.

12.—THE CHOICE OF A SERVANT.*

A FARMER'S wife was in need of a maid-servant, so she asked a number of girls to come to her house that she might choose the one that seemed most likely to suit her. Now, when the farmer's man-servant heard what his mistress was going to do, he said to her, " I will show you how to choose a good one."

" Very well," said the farmer's wife.

So the man-servant laid a besom across the path by which the girls had to come to the house, and he and his mistress watched them as they came near.

The first girl who came kicked the besom aside. Then the farmer's man said, " She's an idle slut, and can't bend her back."

The next girl who came jumped over the besom, and the farmer's man said, " She won't do; she'll skip her work."

The last girl who came picked the besom up and reared it up in a corner out of the way. Then the farmer's man said, "That's the girl for me ; she'll be careful, industrious, and tidy."

So the third girl was chosen.

* From North Derbyshire. Compare Grimm's " Brides on their Trial," No. 155.

13.—A DREAM OF HEAVEN.*

A GIRL called Ann Brown who had been very ill fell into a trance, and it was believed that she was dead. When her body had been laid out for ten hours her mother went into the room where she lay to kiss her, and thought that she felt her daughter's breath warm upon her cheek. Then she fetched the clergyman, and he took a small piece of looking-glass and held it over her mouth to see whether it was steamed by her breath. In this way he found that the girl lived. So he called all the family into the room and told them to stand round the bed. He sat at the head of the bed and took one of the girl's hands into his own, and after a while she opened her eyes, and gave three groans.

Then the clergyman said to her, " Now tell us where you have been."

So after a while the girl opened her eyes and said, " I have been all the way to heaven, and the first to meet me was the Devil, who held in his hand a black book, and the letters in it were written in crimson. The Devil asked me to write my name in the book, and follow him. But I said ' Get thee hence, Satan,' and went further on my way. Next I saw an angel dressed in pure white, who took my hand, and led me on a path as soft as down and as white as snow, until we came to the gate of heaven. And over the gate was written ' Behold the Lamb.' As we came near to the gate it flew open, and the Lord came out and took me in. Then the Lord led me to a place which was full of girls like myself, and after that he took me into another place which was full of soldiers that had spears and bayonets, and the bayonets had seals on them. After this another angel came and took me away from the Lord and led me into another place, which was full of infants singing. I saw the throne of God, which was all bright and shining, but

* From Eckington, in Derbyshire.

they would not let me see God himself. After I had seen the throne the Lord came to me again, and took my hand and said, 'It is God's wish that you go back to the earth for a little while longer.' Then I said to the Lord, 'Let me stay here.' But the Lord answered, 'You have served me faithfully from a child, and it is my desire that you go back to the world.'"

14.—THE ENDLESS TALE.*

ONCE upon a time there was a king who had a very beautiful daughter. Many princes wished to marry her, but the king said she should marry the one who could tell him an endless tale, and those lovers that could not tell an endless tale should be beheaded. Many young men came, and tried to tell such a story, but they could not tell it, and were beheaded. But one day a poor man who had heard of what the king had said came to the court and said he would try his luck. The king agreed, and the poor man began his tale in this way: "There was once a man who built a barn that covered many acres, and that reached almost to the sky. He left just one little hole in the top, through which there was only room for one locust to creep in at a time, and then he filled the barn full of corn to the very top. When he had filled the barn there came a locust through the hole in the top and fetched one grain of corn, and then another locust came and fetched another grain of corn." And so the poor man went on saying "Then another locust came and fetched another grain of corn" for a long time, so that in the end the king grew very weary, and said the tale was endless, and told the poor man he might marry his daughter.

* From Nottinghamshire.

15.—THE CLEAN FAIRY AND THE DIRTY FAIRY.*

ONCE upon a time a dirty fairy stole a little girl and took her to a hill in which she lived a long way off. When the little girl had been there some time the dirty fairy went out one day, leaving the little girl at her house in the hill, and telling her that she must put many thousands of pins straight upon a paper before she came back.

Then the little girl began to cry because she saw that she could not put the pins straight before the dirty fairy came back. Whilst she was crying a clean fairy came into the house in the hill with a wand in her hand, and said, " Why do you cry ? "

The little girl said, " I've all these pins to put straight before the dirty fairy comes back, and I can't do it."

" Don't cry," said the clean fairy, " and I will put them straight for you."

Then the clean fairy passed her wand across them, and they became straight in a moment.

So the little girl waited until the dirty fairy came back.

When the dirty fairy came back, and found that the pins were all put straight she said " Well, never mind, I'll set you a job to-morrow that you can't get done."

So the next day she gave the little girl twice as many needles as she had given her pins to put straight on the paper. And then when the dirty fairy had gone the little girl cried and the clean fairy came as before, and put the needles straight with her wand. And as soon as the dirty fairy had come back she said to the little girl, " Let me see the needles," and she saw that they were all in their places. When the dirty fairy saw that, she said, " I'll set you a job that I know you can't get done."

So the next day the dirty fairy brought a great paper full of beads of many kinds, and told her to thread them in a certain way that was very hard to do. But the clean fairy

* From Nottinghamshire. Compare Grimm's Tales, 13, 14, 55.

came as before and threaded all the beads by waving her wand across them.*

16.—THE BLACKSMITH. WHO SOLD HIMSELF TO THE DEVIL.†

THERE was once a blacksmith who had neither fire nor iron for his forge, and because things did not go according to his mind—

> He ripped and he tore
> And he cursed and he swore.

One day as he was grumbling about his want of work, a man, who was dressed in black, came to see him, and said to him, "What dost thou want?"

The blacksmith answered, "I want nought but iron and stuff for my fire."

The man in black said, "If thou wilt sell thyself to me thou shalt want nought for seven years."

So the blacksmith agreed to sell himself, and when he got back to his forge he found there was as much coal and iron there as he wanted, so that he had plenty of work and plenty of money for seven years. But when the seven years were ended he was down-hearted, for then the devil came for him, and made a great hole in his garden and put a bridge over the hole. Then he said to the blacksmith, "Step on this ring," meaning on the bridge, for he wanted the blacksmith to fall into the hole and break his neck. But the blacksmith defied the devil, and said, "I won't, take all thy coal and iron back to hell with thee." So the devil went and left the man as poor as he found him.

When the blacksmith got back to his forge he found it was empty, but he vowed that he would go without fire, iron, or coal before he would have ought to do with the devil again.

* The story does not end here, but my informant has forgotten the rest.
† From Calver, in Derbyshire.

17.—THE MAN THAT STOLE THE PARSON'S SHEEP.*

THERE was once a man who used to steal a fat sheep every Christmas. One Christmas he stole the parson's sheep, and his son, a lad about twelve years old, went about the village singing—

> My father's stolen the parson's sheep,
> And a merry Christmas we shall keep,
> We shall have both pudding and meat,
> But you moant say nought about it.

Now it happened one day that the parson himself heard the boy singing these words, so he said, " My lad, you sing very well; will you come to church next Sunday evening and sing it there ? "

" I've no clothes to go in," said the boy. But the parson said, " If you will come to church as I ask you, I will buy you clothes to go in." So the boy went to church the next Sunday evening, dressed in the new clothes that the parson had given him.

When the service was over the parson said to the people, " Stay, my brethren, I want you to hear what this boy has to sing, it's gospel truth that he'll tell you," for he was hoping that the boy would confess before all the people that his father had stolen the sheep. But the boy got up and sang—

> As I was in the field one day
> I saw the parson kiss a may ;†
> He gave me a shilling not to tell,
> And these new clothes do fit me well.

18.—THE GLASS BALL.‡

THERE was once a woman who had two daughters, and she gave each of them a beautiful glass ball, of which they were very fond.

---

* From Calver, in Derbyshire.   † Maid. O. N. *mær*, acc. *mey*.

‡ From Norton, in Derbyshire. A story which bears a considerable resemblance to this is given in Henderson's *Folk-Lore*, 1879, p. 349.

As they were playing together one day one of the girls tossed her ball over the wall into the next garden. Now the house which stood in this garden belonged to a fox—a most queer and unsociable fox—who would not talk to his neighbours.

The girl that had tossed her ball over the wall was very much afraid of this fox, but she was very fond of the glass ball, so she said to herself, " I must not lose my ball without first trying to get it back."

So she bravely walked up to the fox's house, but she knocked at the door rather timidly. The fox opened the door himself, and she told him how she had lost her glass ball in his garden, and asked him if she might fetch it out.

" You can have your ball," said the fox, " if you will come and be my housekeeper for a year, but you shall not have it if you won't."

As there was no other way of getting the ball back the girl agreed to live in the fox's house for a year, and she was very comfortable and happy there; but she saw very little of the fox, because he went out early every morning and came back late at night.

Now before the fox went out as usual one morning he called the girl to him and said to her, " I am going away for a little time. While I am away there are five things which you must not do: you must not wash up the dishes, or sweep the floor, or dust the chairs, or look into the cupboard, and you must not look under my bed."

The girl promised that she would not, and away went the fox. But as soon as the fox had gone she began to wonder why he had forbidden her in this way, and she said to herself, " I will see what will happen if I don't do as he tells me."

So first of all she washed up the dishes, and as soon as she had done that a great bag full of copper fell down before her.

" Very good," said the girl.

Next she swept the floor, and as soon as she had done that, down fell a bag full of silver.

c 2

" Better still," said the girl.

Next she dusted the chairs, when down fell a bag full of gold.

" That's just what I want," said the girl.

Next she looked into the cupboard, and there was her glass ball !

" Oh, you don't know how glad I am," she said, and clapped her hands.

Last of all she went up stairs and looked under the bed, and there was the fox ! !

She was almost frightened to death, and she ran downstairs, through the garden, and up the town street, and came to a lane, and at the top of the lane she met a horse, and she said to the horse—

　　　　" Horse of mine, horse of mine,*
　　　　If you meet a man of mine,
don't say that I've passed by."
　　　　And the horse said, " I will not."

A little further on she met a cow, and said—
　　　　" Cow of mine, cow of mine,
　　　　If you meet a man of mine,
don't say that I've passed by."
　　　　And the cow said, " I will not."

A little further on she met a mule, and said—
　　　　" Mule of mine, mule of mine,
　　　　If you meet a man of mine,
don't say that I've passed by."
　　　　And the mule said, " I will not."

A little further on she met a dog, and said—
　　　　" Dog of mine, dog of mine,
　　　　If you meet a man of mine,
don't say that I've passed by."
　　　　And the dog said, " I will not."

* My informant said, " horse of mine, horse of *thine*," and so on throughout.

A little further on she met a cat, and said—
> " Cat of mine, cat of mine,
> If you meet a man of mine,
don't say that I've passed by."
> And the cat said, " I will not."

Last of all she met an owl, and said—
> " Owl of mine, owl of mine,
> If you meet a man of mine,
don't say that I've passed by."
> And the owl said, " I will not."

But the fox had followed the girl, and he came to the same lane, where he met the same horse, and said to him—
> "Horse of mine, horse of mine,
> Hast thou met a maid of mine ? "
> And the horse said, " She's just passed by."

Next he met the same cow, and said to her—
> " Cow of mine, cow of mine,
> Hast thou met a maid of mine ? "
> And the cow said, " She's just passed by."

A little further on he met the same mule, and said—
> " Mule of mine, mule of mine,
> Hast thou met a maid of mine ? "
> And the mule said, " She's just passed by."

A little further on he met the same dog, and said—
> " Dog of mine, dog of mine,
> Hast thou met a maid of mine ? "
> And the dog said, " She's just passed by."

A little further on he met the same cat, and said—
> " Cat of mine, cat of mine,
> Hast thou met a maid of mine ? "
> And the cat said, " She's just passed by."

Last of all he met the owl, and said—
> " Owl of mine, owl of mine,
> Hast thou met a maid of mine ? "
> And the owl said, " She's just passed by."

"Which way did she go?" said the fox. The owl answered, "You must go over that gate, and across that field, and behind the wood you will find her."

Away ran the fox, over the gate and across the field, and into the wood, but neither the fox, the girl, or the glass ball have ever been heard of since.

19.—THE HEDGE PRIEST.*

An Irish parson was walking in Derbyshire one day when a heavy storm came on, and he had to take shelter under a tree. Two young gentlemen and two young ladies were also taking shelter under this tree. The parson saw that they all looked very sad, and he asked them what made them look so miserable. They said, "We are all on our way to church to be married, but the storm has hindered us, and we are afraid it is now too late."

"If that is all," said the parson, "I can marry you."

They gladly agreed, so the parson took his prayer-book out of his pocket and married them at once. After he had said his marriage service he repeated these lines over each couple:

> Under a tree in stormy weather
> I married this man and maid together;
> Let him alone who rules the thunder
> Put this man and maid asunder

20.—THE BOY AND THE PARSON.†

A parson was once walking on the moors when he met a boy who was getting heather to make besoms. The parson said, "Come, my boy, can you tell me what o'clock it is?"

---

* From North Derbyshire. I have supplied the title of the story. Halliwell gives "hedge marriage" as Northern English for "a secret, clandestine marriage."   † From Calver, in Derbyshire.

The boy said, " I can't."

" Well," said the parson, " do you think it's twelve ? "

" It can't be no more," said the boy.

" Well," said the parson, " do you think it's one o'clock."

" It can't be no less," said the boy.

" You're a queer lad," said the parson, " can you read ? "

" No," said the boy.

" Well," said the parson, " how do you get your living ? "

" Way," said the boy, " we mak besoms,* and sell 'em ; and how dost thou get thy living ? "

" Why," said the parson, " I'm a parson."

" Way," said the boy. " Thou gets thy living by saying thy prayers, and I get mine by making besoms. Every man to his trade."

21.—THE PYNOTS IN THE CRABTREE.†

A NUMBER of pynots‡ fought in a crabtree so fiercely that their beaks struck fire and set the tree ablaze. Then roasted crabs fell to the ground, which children picked up and ate.

22.—THE MINISTER AND THE FAIRIES.§

A METHODIST minister once lost his way on the moors. So he asked for a night's lodging at an old house that he passed. The people in the house told him that he might stay, but they said that the house was haunted by spirits, and he might find trouble in the night.

The minister sat downstairs awhile, and then went to bed without his supper. He had not been long in bed before he heard a noise in the house like pots rattling. And he heard

---

* Pronounced *bazooms.* † From Norton, in Derbyshire.
‡ Magpies. § From Calver, in Derbyshire,

the footsteps of somebody walking towards the stairs, and a voice calling, " Armaleg, come to thy supper."

When the hungry minister heard the word "supper" he got out of bed and went downstairs, and there he found a great supper laid out on the table, and many beautiful men and women sitting round it. So he took his place amongst them and said, "I always say grace before meat." So he shut his eyes, and amongst the words of the grace that he said were these : "devils, fear and fly." And then when he opened his eyes the company, the table, and the supper had all gone.

23.—THE WIGGIN STICK.*

ONE night a man came to a toll-bar with a wiggin stick in his hand, and wanted to go through. But the old woman who kept the gate would not open it, so he struck the gate with the wiggin stick. Thereupon it immediately flew open and let him go through, as well as some others who were waiting behind. When the old woman saw this she rushed out of the house, and pointing her hand at the man with the wiggin stick said, " Away wi' thee, thou old devil, wi' thy witch wiggin ! "

24.—THE YOUNGER BROTHER'S DUTY.

AT Holmesfield, in Derbyshire, there were two brothers who lived together, but could not agree. As they were quarrelling one day in the house† the younger brother heard sounds of music in another room. He went into the room

* From Calver, in Derbyshire. The wiggin, rowan, or mountain ash is well known as a reputed protection against witchcraft.

† Cartledge Hall, a little to the south of the village of Holmesfield. This house, which is now occupied as a farmhouse, contains some fine oak carving and pargetted ceilings. It stands opposite to another old house.

from which the sounds came, but he could see nothing, though he could still hear the music. But a voice in the room spoke to him and said, " Thy duty is to leave this place and build a house elsewhere." The voice was the voice of a fairy, so he took the advice which he heard and built a house opposite to his elder brother's house, and spoilt his elder brother's view.

25.—BYARD'S LEAP.*

AT Newmarket, near Market Rasen in Lincolnshire, there once lived a witch who was a great trouble to the farmers in the neighbourhood. They bore it for a long time, until one of them made up his mind to stand it no longer. So he went to the wise man and asked him what he was to do to get rid of her.

The wise man said, " Turn all your horses out of the farm-yard, and drive them to the pond. And when they are drinking throw a stone into the water, and take notice of the horse which is the first to lift up its head. You must mount on his back, and in the night you must call at the hut where the witch lives and ask her to get up behind you and ride. But you must take a dagger with you, and keep it sticking out, so that when the witch leaps upon the horse she may cut her arm."

So the farmer did as the wise man had told him, and took all his horses to the pond. Now it happened that the first horse to lift up its head when the farmer threw a stone into the water was a blind one called Byard.† So the farmer leaped on Byard's back, and the same night he rode straight to the hut where the witch dwelt, and knocked at her door.

---

* From Nottinghamshire. Compare the next tale, and " The Witch and the Ploughman," *post*, p. 44. And see *Choice Notes from Notes and Queries*, 1859, p. 131.

† The word is pronounced Byard, and not Bayard. I am told that white horses are more frequently blind than those of any other colour.

"Mother," said the farmer, " I have come to take thee for a ride, so get up behind me."

So the witch, whose finger nails were very sharp and long, tried to leap up behind the farmer. In doing so she tried to catch hold of Byard with her finger nails, but she fell back twice, and each time that she fell back Byard leaped seven yards forward. At the third leap the witch clung fast to Byard behind, but she grazed her arm against the dagger which the farmer wore by his side. As soon as her arm began to bleed she lost all her power as a witch, and the country was no more troubled with her.

Byard's footprints are still to be seen in the place where he leaped three times. Whoever farms the land where they are is told to keep them clean and never to plough them up. And so they are carefully preserved to this day.*

26.—THE DEVIL'S DITCH.†

NEAR "Byard's Leap "‡ in Lincolnshire is a place called the Devil's Ditch, which was made in this manner a very long time ago. There was a man who wanted to make a road, and whilst he was considering what to do, one came to him and said, "Take thy horse and ride quickly from the place where thou wouldest have the road begin to the place where thou wouldest have it end. But beware that thou dost not

---

* This keeping clean of Byard's footprints, and also his white colour, may remind the reader of the custom known as the "Scouring of the White Horse," which is, or until lately was, kept up at Uffington, in Berkshire. It is also interesting to notice that the colossal figure carved on the chalk of the hill at Uffington represents a horse in the act of galloping. Another account of "Byard's Leap" states that if anyone fills the footprints up they are always empty next morning, that the horse was black, and that the footprints are kept clean by one particular person. See the next tale. A field on the hill-top at Alice Head in Ashover, Derbyshire, is known as White Horse Field.

† From Nottinghamshire.

‡ See the preceding tale.

turn round or look back." So one night the man took his horse and rode quickly over the ground where he wished the road to be, and as he went on the road was made behind him. But just before he reached the end he turned round and looked back. Now in the place where he turned round is a ditch called the Devil's Ditch, which can never be filled up, for as often as they try to fill it during the day so often is it dug out again during the night.*

27.—THE HEN-PECKED HUSBAND.†

THERE was once a poor husband that was ruled by his wife. One day she tormented him so much that he made up his mind to leave her and go into another country. So he set out on his way, and he had not gone far before he came to a farmhouse which stood by the road side. Just as he was passing the door a cock crowed, and he thought the bird said, " Women are masters here ! " He went a few miles further, and came to another farmhouse. As he went by a cock crowed again, and he thought the bird said, " Aye and everywhere ! " Then said the husband, " I will go back and live with my wife, for now I am certain that women are the rulers of men."

---

* According to Leo the Old English *die* " certainly means *agger*, but not in the sense of an isolated heap or an abrupt conical elevation like *hláw*; it is rather a continuous, protecting dam." This story is valuable as giving a satisfactory explanation of such place-names as Grim's Dyke (Grimes díc), for it is evident that Grim represents the Titan, giant, or divine being who in the popular belief made the road and the ditch. The prehistoric road, with its raised banks, or the ancient mound, was believed to be the work of supernatural beings, not malignant spirits, but kindly, who became the helpers of man on the sole condition that their work should be done in secret. We may compare the Old English *enta die*, and *enta hláw*, a dike and a mound made by the giants.

† From Norton, in Derbyshire.

28.—THE GIRL WHO WENT THROUGH FIRE, WATER, AND THE GOLDEN GATE.*

A CERTAIN man and his wife had an only child and she was a girl. This girl was beloved by her father, but hated by her mother. When the girl was about eight years old her father died, and then the mother thought that she would revenge herself upon the girl. So she made her do all the hard work in the house, and gave her many cruel tasks.

One day the mother sent the child to fetch something which lay beyond three fields that were bewitched. When the child drew near to the first field she saw that it was covered with fire, and she stood still at the edge of the field and dare not cross over it. As she stood there trembling with fear and weeping, a beautiful fairy appeared to her and said, "Fear not, for I will help thee."

Now the fairy carried a wand in her hand, which she waved across the field of fire, so that it ceased to burn, and the child went over. But after she had gone a little further on her way she came to a field which was covered with water, and could not get across. Then the beautiful fairy came near to her again as she wept, and waved her wand over the water, which rolled back on either side, so that she walked straight through the midst. So she went on her way again until she came to a house with a golden gate, which she could not open or get through. Then, as before, the fairy came with her wand and opened the gate. And when she had opened the gate, she said to the child, "Wilt thou leave thy cruel mother and come and live with me?" And the child answered: "Yea, I will live with you, for you are so good and beautiful." So she left her cruel mother and went to live with the good fairy in the house with the golden gate.

* From Eckington, in Derbyshire.

29.—THE BROKEN PITCHER.*

ONCE upon a time there were two sisters, one called Orange and the other Lemon. Their mother loved Lemon much more than Orange, and made Orange do all the hard work in the house, and fetch water from the well every day. One day Orange went to the well as usual, taking her pitcher with her, and as she was stooping down to fill it with water the pitcher fell out of her hand into the well and was broken. Then Orange was very grieved and dared not go home; so she sat down on the grass and cried. After she had cried awhile she looked up from the ground and saw a beautiful fairy standing near her. And the fairy said, "Why dost thou cry, little Orange?"

Orange said, "Because I have broken our pitcher, and mother will beat me."

"Dry up thy tears," said the fairy, "and see, I live in the well and know all about you, and I will help you, because thou art such a good little girl, and so ill used."

Then the fairy struck the ground, and the pitcher came back out of the well sound and whole, and just as it was before, except that it had arms and legs.

"See," said the fairy, "this little pitcher shall always be thy friend, and now it will walk home with thee and carry the water itself. Go home now, tell it to nobody, and be a good little girl." Having said this the fairy disappeared down the well.

After this Orange soon dried up her tears, and, taking hold of the pitcher's hand, she and the pitcher walked home together. But when they got to the door of her mother's house the arms and legs of the pitcher were gone. Then Orange took the pitcher into the house, and, remembering what the fairy had said, told what had happened to nobody.

The next morning Orange awoke very early, as she always

* From Sheffield.

did, and said to herself, "How tired I shall be before night comes, for there is so much work to do in the house." So she got up, and when she came downstairs she found the pitcher, with its arms and legs on, sweeping the kitchen and doing all the hard work, and ever after the pitcher was her faithful and helpful friend.

30.—THE MAID WHO WANTED TO MARRY.*

A young Irish girl wanted to marry a young Irishman, so she went to Spinkhill to pray. When she had got very near to the church she knelt down behind a hedge and said : " O, holy mother, can I have Patrick ? " An old man, who was behind the hedge, heard her question and said, " No, thou can'st not." But the girl said, " Thee be quiet, little Jesus, and let thy mother speak."

31.—THE FAIRY AND THE RING.†

THERE was once a wicked king who lived in a large castle which stood on a high hill in a lonely wood, and he had a son who was as wicked as himself. The castle was a very long way from any other house, and nobody ever ventured too far into the wood for fear of being caught by the king

---

* This tale, which comes from Eckington, in Derbyshire, is identical with Grimm's "Maid of Brakel," No. 139. In a note to the story Grimm says, " In Hanover it is told that as the maid was praying to God to give her some sign, a shepherd who had been listening to the whole prayer behind a hedge threw an old shoe over it, for which she thanked God in great delight." As Grimm's notes were not translated into English till 1884 it is clear that there has been no borrowing from him. There is a Roman Catholic church and college at Spinkhill, which is situated in Eckington. I heard the tale myself more than twenty years ago.

† From Sheffield.

or his son, because they were very cruel, and kept prisoners at the castle. One fine day a pretty maid, who had been wandering about the wood, lost her way; but after a time she came in sight of the castle. As darkness was coming on she began to get frightened, and ran up to the castle to enquire her way home. When she got there she knocked at the door, which was opened by a very rough-looking servant.

"Can you tell me my way home?" said the maid.

"No, I can't," said the rough-looking servant; "but I'll fetch my master."

So the servant slammed the door, and went away, and soon after a strong, wicked-looking man came down and said to the maid, "You are a long way from home, and it is dark, so you can't go back now, but follow me, and you shall have a night's lodging."

So the maid followed him, and he led her through a long, dark passage, which brought them to a dimly-lighted room, which was beautifully furnished. There were two servants in the room, and the wicked-looking man, who was the king, told them to give the maid some supper, and then show her to her bedroom. So when she had eaten her supper she was taken into her bedroom, and left alone.

The bedroom was very comfortable, but she began to think about home, and how troubled her father and mother would be about her. "I wonder what will become of me," she said to herself. "I don't like that big, rough man; and oh! it is very lonely here." Then the tears began to fall from her eyes, and she sobbed and could not sleep.

The next morning, when the maid came downstairs, she met the king and his son, and they asked her to take breakfast with them; but she refused, and said, "I want to go home to my father and mother, for they will be grieved about me."

Then the king was angry, and would not let her go, but told the servants to lock her up in a room until they had finished breakfast. After breakfast was done the king and his son went into the maid's room, and she said to them, " I pray you let me go home."

But the king said, "You shall not go home, for I want you to marry my son."

But the maid said, " I will not marry him," and though the king asked her again and again, and offered her all sorts of presents, she still refused.

Then the king grew very angry, and ordered her to be locked up in one of the rooms of the castle until she consented, and to be fed on bread and water. And he said, " Unless you will marry my son you will be put to death."

So when the maid found herself locked up alone she began to cry bitterly, and call for help. And as she was crying she heard a slight tapping at the little window of her room. On looking up she saw a beautiful woman standing on a large stone which projected out of the wall. The beautiful woman asked the maid why she wept. The maid said, " I am a prisoner in this castle, and to-morrow I am to be killed because I will not marry the king's son."

But the beautiful woman said, " Weep no more, but follow me." Then she came through the window, opened the door, and led the way down a dark passage that brought them to the gates of the castle, which were lying open. They walked through the gates unseen by anyone, and the maid found that she was once more in the wood in which she had lost her way.

Soon after the maid had gone, the king sent one of his servants up to the room in which she had lain, to ask her if she had changed her mind, and was ready to marry his son. But when the servant entered the room he found that she had gone. Then the king was very angry, and fetched his dog, and began to search for her in the wood.

When they got out of the castle the maid asked the beautiful woman what her name was, and thanked her for her great kindness. The beautiful woman said, " I am a fairy, and heard thee calling for help, so I came to help thee. But now I must leave thee here."

But the maid was troubled at these last words, and said, "I don't know which way to go. Wilt thou not show me my way home?"

Then the fairy gave her a ring, and said, "See, take this ring, and tie a piece of ribbon to it. Then hold it in front of thee, and it will lead thee home. But take care of it, for if thou shouldest lose it thou wilt lose thy way again, and the king will overtake thee." Then the fairy suddenly disappeared.

When the fairy had gone the maid was very sorry, but she did as the fairy had told her and followed the ring, which floated before her in the air.

Thus the maid walked on, the ring going before her; but after a while she saw some pretty flowers growing in the wood, and stopped to gather them.

Whilst she was gathering the flowers she lost the ring, and could not find it again. So she walked on without the ring, when she came to a river, and wondered how she was to get across.

As she stood wondering by the river side, she heard a dog barking, and also the voice of a man shouting, which she knew to be the king's voice. Then the maid was very frightened, and said to herself, "The fairy told me to take great care of the ring, and that if I lost it I should lose my way, and the king would overtake me. Now I shall be taken back to the castle." And again she wept as though her heart would break.

As she was weeping she heard the voice of one who was singing sweetly, and on looking round she again saw the same fairy who had delivered her from the castle. The fairy said, "Hast thou lost the ring that I gave thee?"

The maid said, "I stopped to gather some flowers, and then I lost the ring. And now I do not know which way to go, or how to cross the river, and the king and his dog are searching for me."

Then the fairy was angry, and said, "Thou hast been careless, and unmindful of what I told thee. But I will

D

have pity on thee and give thee another ring. Follow it, and it will lead thee home." Then the fairy disappeared.

By this time the king and the dog had got close up to her, but the maid followed the ring, which led her straight to a bridge which crossed the river. Then she went over the bridge and found that she was close to her own home. When she got home she found that her father and mother had been greatly troubled, and wished to know everything that had happened. So she told them all that had happened, and how the fairy had saved her.

32.—THE WOODMAN AND THE HATCHET.*

ONE day a woodman was told by his master to cut down some trees that stood near a very deep river. The woodman, however, had lost his hatchet, so he went and borrowed one from a neighbour. And so he walked along the river side until he came to the trees which his master had told him to cut down. So he began to chop at the first tree, but before he had struck many blows the head of the hatchet flew off and fell into the deep water, so that the poor woodman could not get it out again. The woodman was very much troubled about this, because the hatchet was not his own, and as he stood fretting over his loss by the river side a little fairy man appeared on the top of the water, and walked up to him, and asked him what he was fretting about. The woodman said, "I've lost my neighbour's hatchet head in this water, and I can't get it out."

The fairy said, "Where did it fall in?" and the woodman showed him the place.

"Give me the shaft," said the fairy.

So the woodman gave him the shaft, and he threw it into the water in the place where the head had fallen in.

* From Sheffield. Compare the story of "Mercury and the Woodman" in *Æsop's Fables*, which has some resemblance to this. This story contained a verse or two, which my informant cannot remember.

"Keep your eyes fixed on the spot where the shaft fell in," said the fairy, "and the hatchet will rise up out of the water with the head on, just as it was when you borrowed it."

So the woodman did as he was told and kept his eyes fixed on the spot, when shortly he heard a rumbling noise in the water, and after the rumbling had ceased the hatchet appeared in the very place where the fairy had thrown the shaft in. Then the woodman took the hatchet out of the water, but on looking up to thank the little fairy he found that he had gone.

33.—THE IRISHMAN AND THE BULL.*

ONE day as an Irishman was going through a field he suddenly met a bull, which first stamped and snorted and then ran at him. Just as the Irishman was about to mount a wall, the bull helped him over with his horns. The man was very angry when he got down on the other side, and he shook his fist in the bull's face and said, "I'll remember thee!" The next day he had occasion to cross the same field, so he took a good thick stick with him. But when he came to the field he found only two calves there. So he went up to one of the calves and thrashed it unmercifully. When he had done beating the calf he said, "Now, thou can go and tell thy father; he knows all about it."

34.—THE WITCH AND HER BUTTER-MILK.†

ONCE upon a time a farmer and his wife lived at a certain village in Nottinghamshire, and they had a son who got married,

* From Nottinghamshire.
† From Nottinghamshire. Compare "Jack the Butter-milk," *ante*, p. 7

D 2

and brought a beautiful young wife to his father's house. Now in the same village there lived an old woman who was said to be a witch, and the farmer and his wife used to give butter-milk to her. One day when the old woman came for her butter-milk the beautiful young wife said, " We've none to spare; so you must go without it." So the old woman went away without her butter-milk.

Soon afterwards the young wife began to churn, but the butter would not come, and she wondered why it did not. Whilst they were eating their dinner the farmer said, " I wonder why old Sarah has not fetched her butter-milk to-day."

" Well," said the young wife, "an old woman has been here this morning for butter-milk, but I told her we had none to spare."

" Then you can put your churn away," said the farmer, " for you will churn no butter this week. But remember that you don't turn her away again without giving her butter-milk, for she has witched the cream."

35.—THE WIZARD OF LINCOLN.

At a farm in Lincolnshire there had once been a great robbery, and nobody could find out who the thief was. At last the farmer's wife said to her husband, " If you will send for the wizard * of Lincoln, he will tell you."

So the farmer did as his wife had told him, and sent for the wizard, who came in the form of a blackbird. He flew into the crew-yard,† and so frightened the cattle there that a man who was threshing wheat in the barn could hardly keep them out.

Then the blackbird spoke to the farmer, and said " Shall

---

* In Nottinghamshire people say that wizard means "wise man," and wise man, like the O. N. vísinda-maðr, here means soothsayer.

† Farmyard.

I bring the thieves into thy house, or make their shadows appear on the wall ? "

The farmer answered, " Do as thou thinkest right."

He had hardly spoken when one of the farmer's men servants, who had only that very moment begun his work in the fields, walked into the room, and at once passed out.

When he had gone the blackbird said, "That is one of them."

Then he pointed to a shadow on the wall, and the farmer saw that it was the shadow of another of his servants.

"That is the other thief," said the blackbird, and flew away.

Soon after the two men were arrested, and the money which they had stolen was found.

36.—NICORBORE AND HIS MONEY.*

THERE was once a silly man called Nicorbore, who lived as servant in a gentleman's family. One day a sixpence was given to him. He took the coin and buried it in the garden under a gooseberry-bush, "for," said he to himself, " the sixpence will grow bigger." Another servant who had watched Nicorbore burying the sixpence put a shilling in its place. The next day when Nicorbore went to look at his sixpence he found it had grown into a shilling. " I think thou hast grown a bit," he said, " but I think thou'lt grow a bit bigger yet." When he went to look under the gooseberry-bush again he found a half-crown instead of a shilling. " I think thou'lt grow bigger yet," he said, and buried the half-crown again. The next time he found that the half-crown had grown into a five-shilling piece. So he buried the five-shilling piece under the gooseberry-bush again ; but the next time he went to look it had grown into a four-

* From Norton, in Derbyshire.

shilling piece. Nicorbore could not understand this, but he buried the coin as before, and soon afterwards he found it had grown into a shilling, then into a sixpence, and lastly into a threepenny piece. Then he said to the threepenny piece " I'll put thee in my pocket, or thou'lt grow away altogether." *

37.—THE OLD ONE.†

THERE was once a parson in Derbyshire who was very good in visiting his flock and enquiring after their souls. Whenever a parishioner sent for him he always went and spoke words of comfort. One day an old woman sent for him and told him that she was very uneasy in her mind.

When he got to the house he sat down in the kitchen and said : " Way, does ta go to t' sacrament ? "

" Yea," said the woman.

" Way, does ta owe anybody ought ? " said the parson.

" Not a fardin," the woman replied.

" Way, then, what's t' matter wi' thee ? " said the parson.

" Way, t' Owd An' keeps comin'," she said.

" Way, t' next time he comes tell him to go to ——."

* Other tales are told about this Nicorbore. He is said to have drowned a litter of pigs because they had prick ears, for he thought the pigs were young hounds, which should have drooping ears. Another version of the tale given above relates that Nicorbore put the coin into a wall, and that he put it in his pocket when it had grown into a five-shilling piece. There was a tale told about "Nicorbore and Mally Bent that went agatcards all night," but I have been unable to recover any particulars. Nicorbore is said by some to have been a servant who lived at the Oaks in Norton, Derbyshire, but the name itself disproves this. The word Nicorbore evidently contains the O. E. *nicor*, O. N. *nykr*, a water goblin. The final syllable is more doubtful, but it may be Borr, who, according to the Edda, was the father of Odin.

† From Dore, in Derbyshire. In this county the Devil is known as The Old One, The Old Lad, or Old Harry, "Harry" being, I think, the old Norse *harri* or *herra*, lord.

38.—HOB THRUST.*

ONCE upon a time there was a poor shoemaker who could not earn enough to keep himself and his family. This grieved him very much, but one morning when he came downstairs he found a piece of leather which he had cut out already made into a pair of shoes, which were beautifully finished. He sold these shoes the same day, and with the money he bought as much leather as would make two pairs of shoes. The next morning he found that this leather too had been made into shoes, but he did not know who had done it. In this way his stock of shoes kept always getting bigger. He very much wished to know who had made the shoes, so he told his wife he would stay up all night and watch, and then he found Hob Thrust at work upon the leather. As soon as Hob Thrust had finished a pair of shoes the shoemaker took them and put them into a cupboard. Immediately after that Hob Thrust finished another pair, which the shoemaker also took up and put away. Then he made first one pair of shoes and then another so fast that the little shop was soon filled with them, and as there was no more room in the house the shoemaker threw the shoes out of the window as fast as Hob Thrust could make them.

Hob Thrust also worked for farmers in the night. One morning when a farmer woke he found that the hay upon a rough piece of stony ground was newly mown. This had happened several times before, so one day he said he would stay up all night and watch. Then he saw it was Hob

---

* From Dore, in Derbyshire, where the tale is also entitled "Hob Thurst." The *Prompt. Parv.* has "thyrce, wykked spyryte." The first part of this story is identical with the first part of Grimm's tale of "The Elves," No. 39. But it is certain that this tale about Hob Thrust was not borrowed from Grimm, because it has given rise to a proverbial saying in the neighbourhood of Sheffield where knives are made. When a man is heard to boast of the number of knives or other articles which he can make in a day, the rejoinder is, "Ah, tha can mak 'em faster than Hob Thrust can throw shoes out o' t' window." In his capacity as the farmer's friend Hob Thrust reminds us of Thor.

Thrust who mowed the hay; so on the following day he
drove some iron gavlocks and harrow teeth into the ground.
On the next night Hob Thrust came to mow the hay again,
when his scythe struck against a gavlock. He merely said,
" Umph, a dock," and cut through it with his scythe. And
when his scythe struck against a harrow tooth, he said,
" Umph, a dock," and cut straight through it.

39.—THE GIRL WHO FETCHED WATER IN A RIDDLE.*

ONE day a little girl took a riddle to a well to fetch some
water, but the water ran out of the riddle as fast as she
poured it in. Two little robinets who were sitting on a
hedge close by watched her as they twittered their songs.
The birds made such a noise that the girl thought they were
laughing at her, so she said: "Silly robins, how can I carry
water in a riddle?"
    The robinets said:

> Stuff your riddle with moss,
> And daub it with clay,
> And carry your water
> Right away.

But the little girl said, "I shan't, you ugly birds," and
dipped her riddle into the well again. The water ran out of
the riddle again, but the third time the little girl did as the
robinets had told her, when the riddle held the water and
the robinets were pleased.

---

* From Calver, in Derbyshire. Compare the tale of " The Well of the World's
End," printed by Mr. Jacobs in his *English Fairy Tales* (David Nutt, 1890),
p. 215. In this tale a frog, and not robins, advises a girl to stuff her sieve with
clay. According to ancient belief the true-hearted could carry water in a sieve,
and according to modern Indian belief the innocent can take up water in a lump,
like a ball. Grimm's *Teut. Myth.*, pp. 1111, 1112

40.—THE CARD-PLAYER AND THE DEVIL.*

A MAN had been playing at cards with some friends at Totley, in Derbyshire, and was angry because he had lost. And, therefore, he stole the cards and said he would play with the Devil as he went home through a wood. As soon as he had got well into the wood a black man, with cloven feet and horns on his head, came out of the bushes with a small table in his hands, and set it down and said: "I am ready to play." But the man was so afraid that he knelt down and called on God, when the black man disappeared.

41.—THE SONS WHO SALTED THEIR FATHER'S CORPSE.†

A FARMER who had two sons died in harvest time. And because the weather was fine the sons were very busy with their harvesting, and could not spare time to bury him. So one of the sons said to the other, "I'll tell thee what we'll do; we'll take him down into the cellar, and lay him on the milk benk, and salt him." The other son agreed; so they took their father's body into the cellar and salted him, stopping up his ear-holes and nostrils to keep the flies out. About three weeks afterwards it began to rain, and the sons thought they could spare time to bury him. So they went to the parson and told him that their father was dead. The parson was astonished to hear the news, and asked how long he had been dead.

"Three weeks," said the sons.

"Why, he'll stink," said the parson.

---

* From Holmesfield, in Derbyshire. Odin was the god and inventor of dice-playing and gaming, and folk-tales make the Devil play at cards. Grimm's *Teut. Myth.*, 150, 1007.

† From Calver, in Derbyshire. It is still the custom in some parts of that county to lay a plate of salt upon the breast of a corpse previous to burial.

"Nay," said the brothers, "he's as sweet as a pea, for we've salted him."

The parson was so taken aback at these words that he could not speak, and walked away.

42.—TALES ABOUT FAIRIES.*

A CERTAIN widower had six children, but did not know how to manage them, or how to take care of his house. He lay awake all night considering what to do, but when he got up in the morning he found the clothes washed, the bread baked, and the house put in order by the fairies.

A young woman died leaving a baby girl, but before she died her brother promised to take care of the child. But the brother did not keep his promise, so the fairies came and pulled the clothes off his bed. Then the brother fetched the child from his sister's house, and the clothes were not pulled off again.

Another young woman died leaving a baby with her mother, and she was very fond of going from house to house gossiping. One night she put the baby to bed and went out to see a neighbour. When she came back she found the child lying on the hearth dressed in its mother's clothes. She had locked the door, and at first she did not know who had done this, but afterwards she found that the fairies had dressed the child as a warning to the grandmother not to go out gossiping when the baby was put to bed.

43.—THE GOLDEN CUP.†

THERE was once a lady who had one little daughter, and this daughter had a beautiful golden cup. Now one day the lady was going out to visit her friends, and her little daughter

---

* From Calver, in Derbyshire.   † From, Eckington, in Derbyshire.

asked if she might go too. Her mother said, " No, dear, I cannot take you now, but you can have your golden cup to play with until I come back."

When the mother had gone the little girl said to the maid, " Fetch me my golden cup out of the cupboard."

The maid said, " I can't fetch it now, I am too busy."

But the little girl kept asking for the cup again and again, until at last the maid grew angry, and said, " If you ask for it again I'll cut your head off."

But the little girl asked for the cup once more, and thereupon the maid took her into the cellar, got the hatchet, and cut her head off. Then she got a pickaxe and a spade, and dug a hole, and buried the little girl under one of the stone flags in the cellar.

When the mother came back in the evening she said, " Where's baby ? "

The maid said, " I have let her go out for a walk."

" Then go and seek her," said the mother.

The maid went out, and when she came back she said, " I have looked for her everywhere and cannot find her."

Then the mother was deeply grieved, and she sat up all that night, and all the next night. On the third night as she sat alone and wide awake she heard the voice of her daughter outside the door saying, " Can I have my golden cup ? " The mother opened the door, and when her daughter had repeated the question three times she saw her spirit, but the spirit vanished at once, and she never saw it more.

44.—THE WEAVER'S WIFE AND THE WITCH.*

ONCE upon a time a weaver and his wife lived at Sutton-on-Trent in Nottinghamshire. One day the weaver went to Newark to sell his linen, leaving his children in the house, and his wife, who lay ill in bed. Now at that time there

* From Nottinghamshire.

lived at Sutton a witch who had some spite against the
weaver's wife. A short time after the weaver had gone one
of the children heard a noise as of something pattering up
and down stairs. The child opened the door of the bottom
stairs, and there she saw a great ugly cat, which she could
not catch, try as she would. As she was trying to catch it
the cat ran upstairs, sprang upon the bed where the poor
woman lay, and clawed her. But the woman roused herself
and knocked the cat down. Now when the weaver came
back from Newark the children told him about the cat. So
he watched all night in an old lumber-room, for the cat came
in and went out through a broken pane in the window.

One night the cat came in as the weaver was sitting by
the fire, so he picked up a fork and struck her on the cheek.
He then threw her out of doors, believing that she was dead.
But in the morning, when he went to look for the cat's
body, he could not find it. But ever after that the witch
had her face tied up, and she had no more power to do harm
to the weaver or to his family.

45.—THE WITCH AND THE PLOUGHMAN.*

THERE was once a farmer who lived in Nottinghamshire and
kept many servants in his house. Near to his house there
lived a witch, and the farmer often told his servants that if
she asked them to give her anything they should never
refuse. One day the farmer hired a ploughman, and said to
him, "If the old witch up yonder ask thee for ought thou
must give it."

" I shall give the old lass nought," said the ploughman.

One day when he met the witch she asked him to give her
something, and he would not. So the next day, when he
began to plough, his horses would not go, but at last he
coaxed her, and persuaded her to let them go.

* From Nottinghamshire. Compare " Byard's Leap," *ante*, p. 25.

Now this old witch lived by herself in a lonely cabin, and one day the ploughman said he would go and see her. So he knocked at the door of the cabin, and said, "Mother, I've come to take thee for a ride."

The witch said, "Wait till I have suckled my cubs and buckled my shoes, and then I will be with thee." So she suckled her cubs and buckled her shoes and followed him out. But as soon as the ploughman had mounted the horse she turned herself into a hare, and sprang with her claws upon the horse's back. The horse was very frightened, and jumped many feet, but the ploughman killed the hare on the spot.

46.—THE BEWITCHED HORSES.*

ONE day, as a carter was leading his horses along the high road, an old woman came up to him and said, "Please give me a pipe of tobacco." But the carter said, "Nay, thou must buy thy tobacco, like me." So the old woman left him. But after this the horses had not gone many yards before they stood quite still, and could not move an inch. So the carter laid him down by the road side and wondered what he was to do next. As he lay thinking, a stranger came by and said, "What's the matter; why doesn't thou get on?" The carter said, "My horses are bewitched. An hour ago an old woman passed me on the road, and asked me for a pipe of tobacco, and I would not give it her. So she has bewitched them." The stranger said, "You ought to have given her what she asked for, and you were very foolish to refuse. But do as I tell thee. Go to the old woman's cottage, and either beg, borrow, or steal something. And when she comes near thee scratch her arm with a needle, and fetch blood."

So the carter did as the stranger told him, and he called

* From Nottinghamshire.

at a house on the road and borrowed a stocking-needle.
When he got to the old woman's cottage he said to her,
" I've come to buy a penn'orth o' thread, mother." So the
old woman fetched him the thread, and as she was giving it
to him he took the stocking-needle and scratched her arm
from the elbow to the wrist. When he had done this he
paid for the thread, and took the stocking-needle back to
the woman who had lent it him. Then he ran after his
horses, and found that they had started at the very moment
when he drew blood from the old woman's arm.

47.—THE GOOD MAGPIE.*

THERE was once a gentleman who used to ride on horseback
every day. One day he had occasion to call at a house by
the road side, where a woman and her little boy lived.
Whilst he was talking to the woman, he saw that she was
making the oven hot, and the little boy said to him, "Mother's
holing the oven to put me in." But the gentleman thought that
the boy was only joking, so he took no heed, and rode away.
But he had not gone far before a magpie crossed his path,
and kept flying in front of his horse, and would not go away.
So at last he thought that the magpie wanted him to turn
back. So he rode straight back to the house, and when he
got there he found that the woman had gone, and that the
poor little boy was roasting in the oven.

48.—THE OLD WOMAN AND THE FAIRY.†

THERE was once an old woman who lived in the ruins of a
castle that stood in the midst of a great forest. This old
woman used to kidnap girls to help her in many ways, and

* From Nottinghamshire.   † From North Derbyshire.

she taught them witchcraft. Those girls feared the old woman, but one of them—who was very conceited and vain—said to the other girls that she could do anything that the old woman might set her to do, no matter how hard it was. So the other girls told the old woman what the vain girl had said.

"Oh, we'll see about that," said the old woman. So she called the vain girl to her and said, "You must make twenty-one shirts to-day, and be clammed if you can't finish them." Then the old woman went out.

The girl knew that she could not make so many shirts in one day, so she sat crying in the house. But she had not been crying long before she heard a noise in the room, and turning round, she saw a sweet-faced lady, who said, "Why dost thou cry?"

"Because I have to make twenty-one shirts to-day," said the girl, "and I know I can't get them done, and I shall be clammed if I can't."

"We will have them done," said the sweet-faced lady, "before the day is over." So she helped the girl, and the shirts were done before the old woman came back.

So the other girls told the old woman what the vain girl had done. "No matter," said the old woman. "I'll set her a job to do that I know she can't get done." So she called the vain girl to her again, and said, "You must dress* five feather-beds to-day, and be clammed if you can't get them done."

As the girl sat crying the sweet-faced lady appeared to her again, and said, "Don't cry. I am a fairy, and will always be near thee." So the beds were dressed that day by the kind lady's help.

After this the old woman gave the girl harder and harder tasks every day, but she never failed to get them done. Then the old woman, and the other girls, asked her how she

---

* The process consists in taking the feathers out of the beds, putting them into a sieve, and cleaning them with the fingers.

managed to get so much work done, but the sweet-faced lady told her not to make it known, because she was going to help her to get away from the castle to her own home. So the girl would not tell, and in the course of time the kind lady helped her to escape to her own home, where she was received as one from the dead.

49.—THE SHEEP'S HEAD AND DUMPLINGS.*

ONE Sunday morning a farmer's wife had gone to church with her husband and family, leaving one of her sons at home to take care of the house and to keep his eye on a sheep's head and dumplings, which were to be boiled in a pot. When the mother was gone the water began to boil in the pot, and the sheep's head began to swim round after the dumplings, until at last the dumplings flew out of the pot. The boy was much frightened when he saw this. So he left the house with the dumplings lying on the floor and went to the church. Looking in at the door he made signs to his mother to come out. But she took no heed of his beckoning, and answered only by nods and winks. At last the boy grew angry, and shouted loudly into the church, "Thou can'st nod, and thou canst wink, but t' sheep's head's leathered all t' dumplings out o' t' pot." So the mother ran home with her son, and found that it was only the boiling water which had made the sheep's head swim after the dumplings in the pot.

50.—SUGAR AND SALT.†

ONCE upon a time there was a father who had two daughters. Calling them to him one day he said to them, "What is the sweetest thing in the world?"

---

* From Norton, Derbyshire.   † From the East Riding.

"Sugar," said the elder daughter.

"Salt," said the younger.

The father was angry at this last answer. But his daughter stuck to it, and so her father said to her, "I won't keep a daughter in my house who believes that salt is the sweetest thing in the world. You must leave me and seek another home."

So the younger daughter left her father's house and wandered here and there, suffering much hunger and cold, until at last she was befriended by the fairies. As she walked through a wood one day listening to the songs of the birds a prince came hunting for deer, and when he saw her he fell in love with her at once. She agreed to marry him, and a great banquet was prepared at the prince's house. To this banquet the bride's father was bidden; but he did not know that the bride was his own daughter.

Now, at the wish of the bride, all the dishes were prepared without salt. So when the guests began to eat they found that the food was tasteless. At last one of them said, "There is no salt in the meat." And then all the guests said, "There is no salt in the meat!" And the bride's father spoke the loudest of all. "Truly, salt is the sweetest thing in the world," he said; "though, for saying so, I sent my own daughter away from my house, and shall never see her face again." Then the bride made herself known to her father, and fell on his neck and kissed him.

51.—THE HAMMER CALLED "SMILER."*

THERE was once a silly man who broke stones by the road side, and he was so silly that he used to talk to the stones as he broke them.

One day he struck hard at a big stone, but the hammer would not break it.

* From Norton, Derbyshire.

E

"Now, lad," said the silly man, catching his breath, and swinging the hammer back over his shoulder, "I'll bet thee a shilling I *do* break thee."

So he struck the stone with a tremendous whack, but it was not broken a bit.

"Now, then, lad," said the silly man, pulling his coat off, "I'll bet thee a sovereign I *do* break thee, now then."

So he struck the stone with another tremendous whack, but it was not broken a bit.

"Way, lad," said the silly man, pulling both his coat and waistcoat off, and hitching his breeches up with both hands, "I *will* break thee yet. I'll get ' Smiler ' * to thee." (He called his big hammer " Smiler.")

So he lifted " Smiler " up, and brought him down on the stone with all his might. But the stone was not broken a bit.

"Way, lad," said the silly man, "If I can't break thee I can throw thee o'er t' wall."

So he threw the stone over the wall into a field.

52.—THE LITTLE RED HAIRY MAN.†

ONCE upon a time there was a lead miner in Derbyshire who had three sons, and he was very poor. One day the eldest son said he would go and seek his fortune, so he packed up his kit, and took something to eat with him and set off. After he had walked a long way he came to a wood, and being very tired he sat down upon a large stone by the wayside, and began to eat the bread and cheese that he had

* The "silly man" is Thor, and the hammer "Smiler" is the hammer Mjölnir. Compare the tales in the Edda about Thor and his hammer, especially that in which Thor tries to break the head of the giant Outgarth-loki, and fails. The *i* in " Smiler " is long.

† From Wensley, in Derbyshire. Communicated by R F. Drury, Esq., of Sheffield.

brought with him. Whilst he was eating he thought he heard a voice. So he looked about him and saw a little red man coming out of the wood covered with hair, and about the height of nine penn'orth of copper. He came close up to the eldest son, and asked for something to eat. But instead of giving him food the eldest son told him to be off, and kicked his foot out at the little man and hurt him, so that he went limping back into the wood.

Then the eldest son went on his way, and after a long time came home again as poor as he had left.

After the eldest son had returned, the second son said that he would go out and seek his fortune. When he came to the wood he sat down to rest and eat, and whilst he was eating the little red hairy man came out and begged for some food. But the second son went on eating until he had done, and threw the little man the crumbs and bits that were left. Then the little man told the second son to go and try his luck in a mine that he would find in the middle of the wood.

So the second son went to look for the mine, and when he had found it he said to himself, "Why, it's only an old worn-out mine, and I'm not going to waste my time over that." So he set off on his way, and after a long time came home again as poor as he had left.

Now by this time Jack, the youngest son, had grown up, and when the second son came home he said to his father, "I will go now and seek my fortune." So when he was ready he left home in the same way that his brothers had done. And when he came to the wood and saw the stone on the way side, he sat down on it, and pulled out his bread and cheese and began to eat, and in a few minutes he heard somebody say, "Jack, Jack." So he looked about him and saw the same little red hairy man that his brothers had seen. The little man said he was hungry, and asked Jack to give him some of his bread and cheese, and Jack said he would and welcome. So he cut him a good lump, and told him he could have more if he wanted. Then the little man came

close up to Jack and told him that he only wanted to try him
to see what sort he was.

"And now," said the little man, "I will help thee to get
thy fortune, but thou must do as I tell thee."

So then he told Jack to go and find the old mine in the
middle of the wood.

So Jack went, and when he got to the mine he found the
little man had got there before him.

The opening of the mine was inside an old hut, and over
the pit, in the middle of the floor, was a windlass. So the
little man told Jack to get into the bucket, and began to let
him down. So Jack went down, and down, and down, till at
last he came to the bottom, when he got out and found
himself in a beautiful country.

Whilst he was looking round about him the little man
stood by him and gave him a sword and armour, and told
him to go and set free a princess who was imprisoned in a
copper castle in that country. And then the little man threw
a small copper ball on the ground, and it rolled away, and
Jack followed it until it came to a castle made of copper, and
flew against the door. Then a giant came out of the castle,
and Jack fought with him and killed him, and set the
princess free, and she went back to her own home.

When Jack came back the little man told him that he must
go to a silver castle and set another princess free. So the
little man threw down a silver ball, and Jack followed it till it
came to a splendid silver castle, and struck against the door
so loudly that the giant who lived there came out to see what
it was. And then Jack fought with him and killed him, and
set the princess free.

Now some time after Jack had set free the princess in the
silver castle, the little man said that he must now try to set
another princess free who lived in a golden castle. So Jack
said he would, and the little man threw down a golden ball,
and it began to roll away, and Jack followed it until it came
in sight of a magnificent gold castle, and then it went faster
and faster until it struck the castle door, and made the giant

who lived there come out to see what was the matter. Then Jack and the giant fought, and the giant nearly killed Jack, but at last Jack killed the giant, and then went into the castle and found a beautiful lady there. Jack fell in love with her, and brought her to the little man, and he married them, and helped Jack to get as much gold from the gold castle as he wanted. And then he helped Jack and his wife up the mine, and they went to Jack's home.

Jack built a fine house for himself and another for his father and mother. But his two brothers were envious, and went off to the mine to see if they could not get some gold as well as Jack. And when they got into the hut they quarrelled as to who should go down first, and as they were struggling to get into the bucket the rope broke, and they both fell to the bottom of the pit. As they did not come back Jack and his father went to seek them. And when they got to the mine they saw that the sides of the pit had given way, and blocked it up. And the hut had fallen down, and the place was covered up for ever.

EXPLICIT FABULA.

In South Yorkshire when a story-teller has finished his tale
he says :

> My tale's ended,
> T' door sneck's bended ;
> I went into t' garden
> To get a bit o' thyme ;
> I've telled my tale,
> Thee tell thine.

TRADITIONAL REMAINS.

I.—SUPERSTITIONS CONNECTED WITH THE WORLD, THE SUN, MOON, STARS, NATURAL OBJECTS, AND PLACES.

 CHANGE in the moon is said to affect the temper. When sauce, jam, or other liquid compounds are stirred, they must be stirred in the direction in which the sun goes round.

On Easter Sunday people at Castleton, in Derbyshire, used to climb the hill on which the castle is built, at six o'clock in the morning, to see the sun rise. On this day the sun is said to dance for joy at his rising.*

The rainbow denotes that God will not destroy the world by water, but by fire and brimstone. The rainbow is said to have as many colours as Joseph's coat.

It is unlucky to bring eggs into the house after sunset.

If you wish when you see a star shoot your wish will be granted; but you must do this very quickly.

Farmers should sow their seed at the time of the new moon.

If the moon changes on Saturday or Sunday the weather will be stormy during the following month.

A detached piece of rock or stone called "the Cock-

---

* On the Wednesday before Easter Sunday a Derbyshire man said, "I think the sun will hardly be able to contain himself till Sunday." In Derbyshire they say that the sun spins round when he sets on Easter Sunday, and people go out to see this spinning.

crowing Stone," or "Stump John," at Hollow Meadows, near
Sheffield, is said to turn round on a certain morning in the
year* when the cock crows. This rock has the appearance
of a stone pillar. The pillar consists of a large stone standing on the top of another stone. It appears to be about
fifteen or twenty feet high; it stands on the top of a hill and
is a conspicuous object in the landscape. Other stones in the
neighbourhood of Sheffield are known as "cock-crowing
stones." There are also "cock-crowing stones" in the neighbourhood of Ashover, in Derbyshire. There is a stone at
Curbar, in the same county, called "the Eagle Stone," which
is said to turn round when the cock crows.

There are people in Derbyshire who believe that there
was a world before this, that there will be another world
after this, and that then there will be no more worlds.

It is said of a small village called Ompton, in Nottinghamshire, that when God made the world he left a small wagon-
load of people there, and that the village has never grown
bigger since.

It is unlucky to point with your fingers at the moon or the
stars.

In Derbyshire they say that just before the world comes
to an end we shall not be able to tell the difference between
summer and winter. The weather will then be equable—
neither too hot nor too cold. They also say that at the last
day the eye of God will be seen in the sky.

There is a stone called "the wishing stone" in a wood
known as the Faybrick at Ashover, in Derbyshire. If you
sit upon it and wish three times your wish will be granted.

There is an ancient chapel at Hayfield, in the parish of
Glossop. It is said that in the sixteenth century all the dead
in the cemetery which surrounds the chapel rose from their
sleep clothed in golden raiment.

---

* I have not been able to ascertain on what morning. Some people say that
the stone will turn round when it *hears* the cock crow. But this little joke is
a modern perversion of the old lore.

On Kinder Scout,* in the High Peak of Derbyshire, is a pool called " the Mermaid's Pool." It is said that people visit the pool on Easter-eve at midnight, when the mermaid appears and tries to allure her visitors into the water. It is said that several persons have lost their lives in this way, for if the visitor refuses to comply with her request she drags him under the water.

There is a big stone in a farmyard at Crowle, in Lincoln-shire, called " the black stone." If this stone be removed the farmer's cattle will die within a year afterwards. It is said that upon one occasion the stone was removed, when the farmer lost all his cattle and suffered great loss. It was, however, mysteriously brought back.†

There is an old farmhouse in the Peak Forest, in Derby-shire, at which, it is said, there once lived two sisters who loved the same man. To put an end to their rivalry one sister murdered the other, but the dying sister said that her bones would never rest in any grave. And so it happens that her bones are kept in a " cheese-fat " in the farmhouse which stands in the staircase window. If the bones are removed from the vat trouble comes upon the house, strange noises are heard at night, the cattle die, or are seized with illness.

It is said that an underground passage runs between Holmsfield Castle and Holmsfield Hall, in the parish of Dronfield, in Derbyshire.‡ Halfway down the passage is an iron box containing treasure, and upon the lid thereof a cock

---

* "Scout" is the O. N. *skúti*, a cave formed by jutting rocks, M. E. *scoute*, a rock. Grimm mentions the " M. H. G. *kunder*, creature, being, thing, also quaint thing, prodigy." *Teut. Myth.* (Stallybrass), p. 1408. The prodigy in this case may have been the mermaid.

† The Norsemen believed that the family spirit, ármáðr, dwelt in a stone. (Vigfusson and Powell's *Corpus Poet. Boreale*, i. 416). We might render ármáðr " the old one," as to which see tale 37, *ante*, p. 38.

‡ The castle is mentioned in old documents, but no trace of the building, so far as I know, now exists. Traditions about underground passages in connection with old buildings are common in England. This is, no doubt, a traditional remembrance of the Old Norse jarð-hús, " an underground passage opening into a dwelling-house, and used for hiding, or as a means of escape." Vigfusson.

sits which always begins to crow if anyone attempts to go near the box. A similar tale is told about an underground passage between Beauchief Abbey and Norton Church—about two miles apart—in the same neighbourhood. The box which lies in this last-mentioned passage can only be fetched away by a white horse, who must have his feet shod the wrong way about,* and who must approach the box with his tail foremost. The box must be tied to the horse's head and not fastened behind him.

A large swamp called Leachfield, situate about a mile from Baslow, on the road from that village which leads to Sheffield, is said to be the site of a buried village. Some people say that this buried village once belonged to one man who saw it all go down into the swamp one day as he stood on a hill. I am told that near this fen or swamp are two stone circles and two rows of unmistakable stone-built barrows.

In Glover's *Derbyshire* † the following lines occur about this place :

> When Leach-field was a market town,
> Chesterfield was gorse and broom ;
> Now Chesterfield's a market town,
> Leach-field a marsh is grown.

I have heard the last two lines repeated thus :

> Now Leach-field it is sunken down
> And Chesterfield's a market town.

The place is also called Leach Fend, Leys Fen, and Leck Fen. The ground is very swampy; it is covered with coarse grass and rushes, and a sluggish stream runs through it.‡

* I have heard of sheep-stealers who reversed their horses' shoes to avoid detection.

† Vol. ii. p. 86.

‡ This interesting tradition of a buried village suggests lake-dwellings. In the dialect of North Derbyshire a *lache* is a marshy place or fen, being equivalent to the Middle English *lake*, a wet place. See my *Sheffield Glossary*, p. 127. In Wood's *Tales and Traditions of the High Peak*, 1862, p. 204, it is stated that "fragments of rude earthenware" and "pieces of black oak, squared and cut by some instrument," were found here on making a deep ditch.

There is a well at Bretton, near Eyam, in Derbyshire, called Dewric Well, the water of which is said to make any woman who drinks of it fruitful.

Children living at Dore, in the parish of Dronfield, near Sheffield, were afraid to fetch water from a well called Sparken Well,* because, they said, it was haunted by a spirit.

There is a wishing well near Roche Abbey. If you breathe a wish as you go past the well your wish will be granted.

Water that is watched is long in boiling. In East Yorkshire if a kettle boils slowly they say "the kettle is bewitched; it must have a stone in the bottom."

When people cross a stream of water, or stand on the middle of a bridge, they express a wish. In the East Riding of Yorkshire they stand by the side of a brook, spit in it, and wish, taking care to tell nobody what the wish is.

When you first see the new moon you should bow to it three times (some say nine times). It is often said of a man who is unlucky that he has forgotten to bow to the moon, or that he has looked at the new moon through a glass. The first new moon should be seen in the open air.

The "man in the moon" is said to have a bundle of sticks on his back, and it is said that he was put there because he gathered sticks on Sunday.

When you first see the new moon bow to it nine times and wish.

It is unlucky to have your hands empty when you first see the new moon. On that occasion you should turn the money over in your pocket for luck.

When the moon is full girls cut the ends of their hair even, so that it may grow long and thick.

In the East Riding women go out of doors and turn their aprons before the new moon. They then wish something without telling their wish to anybody.

---

* O. N. *spákona*, a prophetess, sorceress. Compare Sparken Hill at Worksop in Notts, and *spákonu-fell*, a local name in Iceland.

With reference to the crooked steeple of Chesterfield
Church, people say that the first pair who were married in
the church were very innocent, and that caused the steeple
to be crooked. They also say that the next innocent pair
who go there to get married will make the steeple straight
again.

It is usual to kill pigs before the full moon, in the belief
that as the moon waxes so the bacon will swell in the pot.
If the pig be killed in the wane of the moon the bacon will
decrease in bulk.

When a star shoots a spirit is going to heaven.

There is a well at Hathersage, in Derbyshire, called Gospel
Well.*

On seeing the first star in the evening say the following,
and wish something :

> Star light, star bright,
> The first star I've seen to-night,
> Would it were that I might have
> The wish I wish to-night.

When the new moon appears put silver, gold, and copper
in your pocket. Put your hand in your pocket, and, looking
up at the moon, turn the money over. After that you will
be lucky for a month.

At Bradwell, in the Peak of Derbyshire, once. lived a man
known as Master John, who was reported to be a wise man,
and whose advice was sought by all the people in the village.
It is said that the ghost of a child who had been murdered
in the village could not be appeased, and so the aid of Master
John was invoked. Master John pronounced the words " In
the name of the Father, Son, and Holy Ghost, why troublest
thou me" and turned the ghost of the child into a large fish.
This fish used to appear, it is said, at a place called the Lum

* " In Cheshire in Mr. M. Kent's grandmother's time, when they went in perambulation, they did blesse the springs, they did read a ghospel at them, and did
believe the water was the better." Aubrey's *Remaines of Gentilisme* (Folk-Lore
Soc.), p. 58.

Mouth, and also at Lumley Pool, in Bradwell, on Christmas Day to people who fetched water from the wells there. When anybody saw the ghost in the form of a fish he would run away, screaming "the fish, the fish."*

When the church at Holme-on-the-Wolds, between York and Hull, was first built the fairies removed the stones by night, so that the builders had to build the church on another site.

Clowne Church, in Derbyshire, was spirited from one side of the road to the other, and that is why it stands where it is.

A long time ago there was a village in the North Riding of Yorkshire called Simmerdale, at one end of which stood a church, and the house of a Quaker woman at the other end. It happened one day that a witch came into the village, and, beginning at the house next to the church, asked for food and drink, but her request was refused. And so she went on from house to house, without getting either food or drink, until at last she came to the Quaker woman's house. There, sitting in the porch, she was regaled with bread, meat, and beer. Having finished her repast, she rose and waved an ash twig over the village, saying:

> Simmerdale, Simmerdale, Simmerdale, sink,
> Save the house of the woman who gave me to drink.

When the witch had said these words the water rose in the valley and covered the village, except the old woman's house. Simmer Water is now a peaceful lake, and on fine clear days people in the neighbourhood fancy that they can see down in its placid depths the ruins of the village and church.†

---

* Compare Wood's *Tales and Traditions of the High Peak*, 1862, p. 183.

† Semer Water or Simmer Lake, is near Askrig, in the North Riding. "It covers, at a medium, 105 acres of land, but as the banks are low, when the feeders are swollen by rains its surface extends to twice that measure. Its greatest depth is 45 feet." Whitaker's *Richmondshire*, vol. i. 412, 414. The legend was told to me by a native of the North Riding now resident in Sheffield.

II.—SUPERSTITIONS ABOUT TREES AND HERBS.

CHILDREN say that if you pluck the little flowers known as bird-eyes the birds will come and pick your eyes out.

If you sleep in a bean-field you will see frightful visions. Colliers say that accidents are most frequent in coal-pits when broad beans are in bloom.* In Yorkshire they say that these sweet-smelling flowers contain the souls of the dead.

Where there is a sweet-briar tree growing in the garden of a house, the mistress, and not the master, of that house must rule, or the tree will not flourish.

A bay-tree in your garden will protect your house, or anything in your farm or grounds, against lightning.

When rosemary grows in the garden the mistress rules the house.

It is unlucky not to have some house-leek growing on your house, or the outbuildings thereof.†

It is very unlucky to burn yew. This tree is held in great esteem, and farmers will not have it cut down if they can help it.

If the trees of a man's orchard blossom out of season death will visit his family.

An old man said that when he was a boy his mother had a superstitious regard for the ivy when growing upon the oak, and that she once thrashed him for destroying some ivy which clung to that tree. She had no objection to ivy being cut when it grew upon a house.

An old tree, or stump of a tree, at the Hagg, in Staveley parish, in Derbyshire, was called a "mandrake tree." If cut or disturbed it was said to make a moaning noise. Its

---

* Compare Terence (*Eun.* 2, 3, 89) *Istaec in me cudetur faba*, this bean will fall on me, *i.e.* I shall have to smart for it.

† An old house at Ecclesall, near Sheffield, is called Thrift House, probably from the plant *thrift*, house-leek, or stone-crop, which may formerly have grown on the roof.

root was said to resemble the human body. It was surrounded by a wall, and people used to visit it out of curiosity. It is said that a ghost used to appear.on.the spot in which the tree grew. The parson was sent for, and he read to it. Then the ghost was "laid," and the "mandrake tree" planted.

If you see a daffodil with its head bending down towards you, it is a sign that you are about to die.

A smell of thyme may always be perceived near a footpath leading from Dronfield to Stubley, in Derbyshire. It is said that a young man murdered his sweetheart there as she was carrying a bunch of thyme.*

People in Derbyshire will not burn elder wood, because, as they say, Christ was crucified on the elder tree.

It is unlucky to burn evergreens, or green plants of any kind.

In the East Riding the bloom of hawthorn is not permitted in the house; "it has such a deathly smell."

When blackberries are over-ripe, and have lost their flavour, the Devil is said to have "cast his club over them."

If you gather fruit on Sunday the Devil brings the fruit back to the tree faster than you can pluck it off.

It is lucky to find four-leaved clover.

When parsley is sown it goes nine times to the Devil before it comes up. Only the wicked can make parsley grow.

It is unlucky to bring any green plant into your house after sunset.

If you have a witch-wiggin tree (mountain ash) in your garden you will never be troubled by the witch.

In the *Sheffield Telegraph* of December 24, 1891, it is said that "The last great gale blew down in the grounds of

---

* Staining Hall, in Lancashire, "has its 'boggart,' according to tradition the wandering ghost of a Scotchman, murdered near a tree, which has since recorded the deed by perfuming the ground around with a sweet odour of thyme." Thornber's *Hist. of Blackpool*, 1837, p. 38, n.

Jordanthorpe,* Norton, a tree with a tradition. It is said to have been planted eighty years ago, 'to keep the witch out of the churn,' . . . . . The people there spoke of the tree as the wiggin-tree." A few days later the Vicar of Wortley, near Sheffield, said, in the same paper, that in his parish the tree is known as the " wickersberry tree."

In Derbyshire it used to be said that a man would be " transported " (perhaps a polite way of saying " kicked out of the parish ") if he cut down a young ash tree. In the East Riding of Yorkshire the seeds of the ash are known as " kitty keys," or " cattle keys."

It is said in Yorkshire that the fairies make their home in foxglove bells.

When a child is born a tree is sometimes planted. At Grainfoot, near Ashopton, in Derbyshire, it is said that three trees were planted on the respective births of three sons. "Two of the sons and their trees attained old age, the third son died in his prime in India. His tree stopped growing, and still remains of stunted growth."

The rose known as the " York and Lancaster rose " is said originally to have grown on a battle-field whereon adherents of the houses of York and Lancaster were killed. The blood of the slain mingling with the dust produced a new variety of rose. This belief is common in Yorkshire and Derbyshire.

It is lucky to find a piece of white heather. If a piece of white heather be given by a man to a woman a declaration of love is intended.

III.—SUPERSTITIONS ABOUT ANIMALS.

WHEN a bee-master dies tins containing funeral biscuits soaked in wine are put in front of the hives, so that the bees may partake of their master's funeral feast. Two kinds of funeral cakes are used, namely, biscuits and " burying cakes,"

* This should have been Lightwood, and not Jordanthorpe.

the latter only being given to the poor. The bees always have the biscuits, and not the "burying cakes." At Eyam, in Derbyshire, a portion of the "burnt drink" and of the three-cornered cakes used at funerals is given to the bees of the deceased bee-keeper.* Sometimes pieces of black crape are pinned upon the hives. It is said that the bees must be told of their master's death, or they will all die. These customs are rarely or never practised now, but they are remembered by old people.

If a bee alights upon your head and stays there you will rise to be a great man in after years.

Bees never ought to be bought; they should be either given or stolen.

An old woman at Ompton, in Nottinghamshire, used to take great notice of bees. She once saw her bees "creeping about in pairs as mourners do" for many days. Shortly after that her daughter died.

If a bee comes into your house a stranger will visit you soon afterwards. If bees swarm on rotten wood a death in the family is betokened.

In the East Riding, when bees were ready to swarm, the new hive was sprinkled with a bottery (elder) branch dipped in sugar and water. When the hive-stand was lengthened the new part was called an *eke*.

In Lincolnshire the first pancake which the farmer's wife fries on Shrove Tuesday is given to the cock in the crew-yard. Old wives cannot be persuaded to fry another cake until one has been given to the cock. The daughter of the house watches the ceremony, and as many hens as come to help the cock to eat the pancake so many years will she remain unwed.†

* See under Section X for "burnt drink," &c.

† For an account of the brutal practice of "throwing at cocks," on Shrove Tuesday, see Hone's *Every-day Book*, 1826, i. 252. This Lincolnshire custom seems to show that the offering of a pancake to the cock was a pagan rite, and that Christian sentiment, to show its contempt for paganism, persecuted the bird in the same way that the wren, once highly venerated, was afterwards hunted and killed.

When a cock crows against the house the coming of a stranger is announced.

It is unlucky for a cock to crow between sunset and midnight. Farmers will kill a cock which crows at this time. When a hen crows like a cock it is a sure sign of misfortune.

If the cock crows when you are going to bed it will rain the next day. If a cock crows on a high building or a high wall the weather will be fine.

Robin redbreasts are called birds of paradise. It was they who went to cover Christ with leaves, touching his blood with their breasts. Hence they have been red ever since.

If a black pigeon settles on your house there will be a death in your family.

On meeting magpies, the following lines are repeated in Nottinghamshire :

> One for sorrow, two for mirth,
> Three for a wedding, four for a birth,
> Five for a parson, six for a clerk,
> Seven for an old man buried in the dark.

If you meet two pynots (magpies) you will prosper; if you meet one it is the worst luck that can happen to you.

When a cock reaches the age of seven he lays an egg.

When a hen wants to sit, an odd number of eggs, usually eleven or thirteen, is put under her. Thirteen is the most common number.

If you burn egg-shells the hens will not lay.

It is unlucky to kill spiders, and it is said that:

> He that would wish to thrive
> Must let spiders run alive.

In the East Riding they say, " Never kill a spider; there is room in the world for us and it."

If you kill the first wasp that comes into your house in the spring you will not be troubled with any more wasps during the year.

Snakes will not come near a raw onion. If you go into a

wood where snakes are, and take a raw onion with you, the snakes will be driven away.

Horses will not go past snakes or adders; they can smell them afar off.

It is unlucky to dream about snakes, which are your enemies. If in your dream you get safely past them you will overcome all your enemies.*

It is lucky to hear corn-crakes at night.

If you kill a beetle or a cockroach it will rain.

If an odd cricket chirp in your house it is a sign of death.

Pigs which are killed between eight and ten of the clock in the morning will weigh more and be in better condition than they would be if killed at a later time of the day.

Take notice of the first lamb which you see in the spring. If it has its tail towards you, you will have bad luck that year; if its head is towards you, you will have good luck.

If a calf has a white streak down the middle of its back it will never thrive.

If you see a yellow frog it is a token of fine weather.

When trouble is about to visit you a bird will come sighing or "tweedling" about you so as to give you warning.

Some farmers believe that pigs can see the wind.

Water which is inhabited by frogs is good to drink.

It is said that toads spit fire, and that they will fly at you if driven into a corner.

The marks below a haddock's neck denote the thumb-marks of Peter when he laid hold of that fish to take out the piece of money.

It is lucky to have swallows' nests about your house, and boys who throw stones at them must be punished. These birds mourn for Our Lord. They are sacred, and must not be destroyed. Cats will not eat robins or swallows.

A story was told in Derbyshire about a cow which supplied

---

* I am told that people sometimes dream that they are walking down a lane full of snakes.

a whole village with milk * during a time of famine. But a witch came and milked the cow through a sieve, whereupon the cow went mad. According to another account it was the witch herself who kept the cow, and went three times a day to milk her, so as to supply the village with milk. One day a stranger came to the village and asked the witch to fill his water-can full of milk. This made the witch so angry that she struck the cow in front of him, and then the cow dropped down dead.

When crickets chirp in your house you will have good luck.

If a white cricket appears on your hearth death is betokened in your family.

When a crow sits on a wall it will rain.

If a raven croaks near your house trouble is near.†

If one sees a black spider death is betokened.

When trouble is about to come upon you, you will hear a noise like the chatter of a magpie, whether a magpie be near or not.

When a man is in trouble a bird will always haunt him. He will see that bird wherever he goes.

It is a sign of death when birds peck at the window-panes.

It is good to see a hawk at a wedding, because it never eats the hearts of other birds.

It is good for a black cat to come to your house; on no account should it be driven away. When you flit or move into another house it is unlucky to take the cat with you. It is all right if the cat follows you of its own accord.

If your cat sits with her back to the fire it is sure to rain.

* This appears to be the cow Audhumbla, mentioned in the Edda, that suckled the giant Ymi, and out of whose dugs ran four rivers of milk. In a perverted form we have here "the early myth of the holy cow—first-born of things, a figure common to Indian and Teutonic fancy." Vigfusson and Powell's C. P. B., vol. i. ci.

† Cleasby and Vigfusson under the word *hrafn* refer to Landnáma, in which it is said that the croaking of ravens "when heard in front of a house betokens death."

It is unlucky for a crow to fly across your path. If it does so you should say:

> Crow, crow, fly out of my sight,
> Or else I'll take thy liver and light.

But it is not unlucky for a solitary crow to cross your path if another person is with you. If you are alone, make the sign of the cross on your left hand. The following lines are also said with regard to crows crossing one's path:

> One for sorrow, two for mirth,
> Three for a wedding, four for a birth,
> Five for heaven, six for hell,
> *   *   *   *

When a robin "tweets" or makes a mournful noise at your window, trouble is about to come upon the house.

If a nurse finds a louse in her head it is a sure sign that her patient is going to die.

If you dream that you are covered with lice there will be an illness, such as a fever, in your family.*

It is lucky to take a horse through your house.

When crows or swallows fly high the weather will be fine.

In the East Riding it is said that Satan was in the *hoofs* of the swine when they rushed down a steep place into the sea.

---

* Women sometimes say that they have such dreams. The notion seems almost prophetic of the germ theory of disease. In January, 1874, a writer in the *Sheffield and Rotherham Independent*, said : "A few weeks ago I saw a woman in a melancholy state, and found upon inquiry that she dreaded something serious was about to happen to a near relative or friend, as she had that day found a big louse in her head, and had done so before her father took his bed never to rise from it again."

In the same newspaper, J. Law, M.D., of Sheffield, wrote a letter bearing date July 13, 1878, in which he said : "About thirty years ago the late lamented Mr. Chesman showed to the Medical Society, of which I was the secretary, a lamprey, or seven-dotted eel, given to him by a patient of his, a woman living in Green Lane. Having long complained of gastric uneasiness she vomited the fish, and was relieved. The woman's theory was that in drinking the river water she had inadvertently swallowed a very young eel, and that it had attained its full growth in her stomach. . . . . The case was looked upon as one of those examples of hysterical malingering which do not surprise medical persons, only because few things surprise those who see them often."

It is unlucky to pull a robin's nest.　If a robin enters your house it is a sign of death or severe illness in your family.

The owl is a bird of ill omen.　If it shrieks near a house at night death is presaged.

·

IV.—WITCHCRAFT.

WITCHCRAFT may be acquired in the following way :—When taking sacrament at church, instead of eating the cake which the parson gives you, save it, and wait until all the people have gone home.　Then walk backwards round the church nine times, looking into every window and door as you go. Then return home, and, as you go, give the cake to the first living thing that you meet, be it dog, cat, or any other animal.*

Witches are dressed exactly like fairies.　They wear a red mantle and hood, which covers the whole body.　They always wear these hoods.†　An old woman living at Holmes-

* In Sheffield and other towns in Yorkshire it was the custom to whip dogs on October 18.　This day was called Dog-whipping Day, and the custom is said to have arisen from the fact that a dog once swallowed the consecrated wafer in York Minster.　See my *Sheffield Glossary*, p. 63.　In Potts's *Discoverie of Witches*, 1613, H. 3 *a* (Chatham Society's reprint), James Device " saith that vpon Sheare Thursday was two yeares, his grandmother Elizabeth Sothernes, alias Dembdike, did bid him this examinate goe to the church to receiue the communion (the next day after being Good Friday) and then not to eate the bread the minister gaue him, but to bring it and deliuer it to such a thing as should meet him in his way homewards.　Notwithstanding her perswasions this examinate did eate the bread ; and so in his comming homeward some fortie roodes off the said church, there met him a thing in the shape of a hare, who spoke vnto this examinate, and asked him whether hee had brought the bread that his grandmother had bidden him, or no ?　Whereupon this examinate answered, hee had not ; and thereupon the said thing threatned to pull this examinate in peeces, and so this examinate thereupon marked himself to God, and so the said thing vanished out of this examinate's sight."

† Compare " Little Red-cap " (Grimm's *Household Tales*, No. 26), Perrault's *Le Petit Chaperon Rouge*, and our " Little Red Riding Hood."　This connection of witches with fairies is very remarkable, and we seem to get here the dress of the ancient priestess who was covered with a mantle.　Compare the Old high German *hœchel*, a witch, and the Old English *hœcele*, a cloak.

field, in the parish of Dronfield, in Derbyshire, who wore "one of those hoods called 'little red riding hoods,'" used to be called "the old witch." The favourite meeting-places of witches are cross-ways, or "four lane ends," or toll-bars, where they bewitch people.

If an old woman comes begging to your door never give her silver. If you do so she will gain some power over you.

There was a wise woman at Killamarsh, near Chester-field, whom people consulted when they were in any difficulty. She could tell a woman where her drunken husband was, and in this, it is said, she was never known to fail.

If you are bewitched get a twig from a tree, cut it in two, and make a cross of it. You should carry this about with you, stitch it up in your dress, or put it under your pillow. By this means you will charm away any harm that the witch may have done to you.

A girl in Derbyshire who was engaged to be married to a young man with light hair met a wise woman, or witch, who told her that she must marry a dark-haired man. She gave the girl a piece of paper, "shaped like half a diamond," in which she pricked three marks with a pin. She told the girl to wear the paper in her bosom for three weeks, after which she would find the name of the dark-haired man written on the paper.

In North Derbyshire the memory is still preserved of people who have sold themselves to the Devil. The names of people who have done so are mentioned. The wise man at Chesterfield was one of them.

A story is told about an old woman at the Hallowes, in the parish of Dronfield and county of Derby, who baked oat-cakes on Sunday, until one Sunday she was burnt to death.

When a horse-shoe is nailed to a stable door to keep witches out the nails must not be driven through the shoe; they should be driven so as to hold the shoe by its sides. Farmers, early in the present century, were very particular about not having these horse-shoes disturbed or removed.

They would almost kill a man if he attempted to remove them.

To keep the witch out of your house let the handles of your brooms be made of wiggin (mountain ash).

Many women in Derbyshire carry about with them a little cross made of two twigs of witch wiggin as a protection against misfortune or witchcraft. It is worn concealed under the dress.

An old woman living at Greenhill, near Norton, in Derbyshire, who was reputed to be a witch, could tell, it is said, who the next person to die in the village would be.

On several occasions a Yorkshire farmer found his horses bathed in perspiration and in a state of terror when he went into his stable in the morning. One night, seeing on his premises a strange cat, he threw a stone at her and broke her leg. The next morning an old woman in the village was found to have her leg broken. It was said that she was a witch who appeared at night in the form of a cat.

Traditions linger in Yorkshire about the presents, such as milk and other food, which had to be made to a witch whenever she applied for them at the door, through fear of being bewitched.

A woman living at Eckington, in Derbyshire, was reputed to be a witch. She always lay in bed till twelve o'clock at noon. It was said that she held communion with the Devil, to whom she had sold herself, and that she had power to make people perform her commands. She once told a man to go to bed, when she wished him to be out of the way, and he immediately obeyed her.

At Laxton, in Nottinghamshire, there once lived a wise man who had power to do almost anything. If a man in the village had quarrelled with his neighbour, or had any spite against him, he went to the wise man and told him what he was to do against his enemy. On one occasion the wise man was told that he must cause a man's legs to be broken off by the knees. This was done, and the poor man walked on stumps till he died.

A woman living at Eyam, in Derbyshire, who was reputed to be a witch, had a bottle of "horse-nail stumps" which she shook and rattled before a person whom she meant to bewitch.*

In Nottinghamshire there was once an old woman whom her neighbours believed to be a witch. She used to take the form of a magpie, and appear to her neighbours in that shape. When she was near to death she called her neighbours together and sang to them this death-song:

> When the Lord takes old women's senses
> He takes them over dikes and fences,
>   Straight away to heaven.
> When the Lord gives old women graces,
> They wear no more witches' faces,
> For the Lord takes them straight to heaven.†

V.—MAGIC, CHARMS, AND DIVINATION.

In Derbyshire it is usual to drive a horse-shoe between two flags or stones near the door of the house, the circular part of the shoe being driven downwards. This is done to keep the witch out.

To see the vision of your future wife sit on a strike in the barn at midnight, when she will walk in at one door and out at the other. A man said that he once saw his future wife, a woman with black hair, in this way. Another man saw a pickaxe and a spade walk through the barn, which betokened that he would remain unmarried. In Derbyshire this charm is tried on St. Mark's Eve.

If a woman's sweetheart is cold to her, or does not visit her when he ought to come, she should take the shoulder-

---

* This is an interesting survival of savagery. When the African soothsayer or sorcerer gives his response he shakes a small gourd filled with pebbles. Macdonald's *Africana*, 1882, i. 44.

† There were more of these verses which my informant cannot remember.

blade* of a lamb, and, as she goes upstairs, say these lines :

> It's not this bone I wish to stick,
> But my true lover's heart I mean to prick ;
> Wishing him neither rest nor sleep
> Until he comes to me to speak.

When she has reached her bedroom she should stick a penknife into the shoulder-blade.

In the East Riding the same charm is practised by striking a fork into an uncooked shoulder of mutton for three nights.

If your lover forsakes you get a lock of his hair and boil it. Whilst it is simmering in the pot he will have no rest.

Divination by the key and Bible is practised in the following way. A key is put into the centre of the Bible with the ring outside. A garter, made of tape, is then tied round the Bible to keep the key in position, and the key is suspended on the fingers of two persons. A question, which must be answered by "Yes" or "No," is then put to the Bible. If the key and Bible turn the answer is "Yes," if they do not the answer is "No." The initial letters of one's future husband's or wife's name may be ascertained thus : Take a Bible, tie it round with your garter--they used to be made of pretty pieces of crochet—and twirl it round with a key inserted in the loop, repeating Ruth's adjuration, "Entreat me not to leave thee," etc.,† the while. Then untwirl it, and, as you do so, repeat the letters of the alphabet. The letters which come next before the stopping of the twirling will be the initial letters sought for.

When divination with the key and Bible is practised in love affairs the following words are sometimes said : "Many waters cannot quench love, neither shall the floods drown it. If a man will give the substance of his house for love yet it will utterly be condemned."‡

---

* *Spatulamancia*, or divination by the shoulder-blade. was an ancient practice. See instances in Grimm's *Teutonic Mythology, passim.*

† Ruth i. 16.

‡ Solomon's Song, viii. 7. I have written down the exact words as given to me. They vary a little from the authorised version.

A man at Holmesfield, near Dronfield, in Derbyshire, said he would raise the Devil. He took a frying-pan and key, and, in the dusk of evening, went to a " four-lane-ends," or cross-way. Many people were assembled to see him perform this feat. The man rattled the frying-pan and the key together, and repeated the lines :

> I raised the Devil, and the Devil raised me,
> I never shall forget when the Devil raised me.

All at once there was a great noise of thunder, in the midst of which the Devil came ; but nobody saw him except the man who had raised him by the key and frying-pan. The man was much alarmed, and falling on his knees he said, " Get thee behind me, Satan, for it is written that thou shalt worship the Lord thy God, and him only shalt thou serve." Then the Devil went away like a flash of lightning.

When charms and divinations are practised, as, for example, when the spirit or form of a future husband or wife is summoned to appear, there comes a rushing wind as the spirit draws near.* The doors shake and knock, and everything rattles. When the knocking and rattling are heard the door should be opened by one of the persons present.

To raise the Devil go to bed saying the Lord's Prayer backwards, and take a mouldy halfpenny and some mouldy cheese with you.

One Good Friday a Derbyshire girl, who was going out for a holiday on the following day, put a singlet † before the fire to dry. As the singlet was drying she saw that a pen-knife was stuck into it, and she also saw in the room the form of the man whom she afterwards married. She kept the knife, and shortly afterwards married the man. One

---

* In Acts ii. 2, when the Holy Ghost appeared " there came a sound from Heaven as of a rushing mighty wind, and it filled all the house where they were sitting."

† A vest, or piece of underclothing worn next the skin. In this case it is said that the girl did not intend to practise divination or magic. In the East Riding the girl sits before the fire on St. Mark's Eve dressed only in her shift. If a man comes at midnight and cuts a hole in the shift " he will marry her and swing for her."

day as she was unpicking something with the knife her husband saw it and said, "Oh, what torture have I suffered on account of that knife !" (He meant that she had used a wicked charm.) He therefore took the knife from her hand, cut a vein in her neck, and killed her.

In 1888 a man and a woman living at Cold-Aston, in Derbyshire, were engaged to be married. The wedding-ring was bought one Saturday, and the marriage was to be celebrated on the following Monday. But, in the meantime, they quarrelled, and the marriage did not take place. On the Monday evening the boys in the village made a straw image of the man, which they burnt in the street opposite to his door, and they also burnt a straw image of the woman opposite to her door in the same manner.*

Lately, at the same place, when a man was " ran-tanned," that is, when a straw image of him was made, and he rode in effigy, the image was taken round the village on three successive nights, and it was burnt on the last night. The carrying round of the image was accompanied by a number of people beating tin cans, and making a great din. It is said that if you carry the image round the village on three successive nights the man cannot " have the law" of you. In this case the man had quarrelled with his wife, and the wife's friends caused the image to be made and carried round.

To meet your future wife or husband count seven stars in the sky on seven successive nights, and on the eighth day the first person with whom you shake hands will be your wife or husband.

The following extract from the *Sheffield Daily Telegraph* of August 18, 1890, describes a charm for recovering a dead body :

"Yesterday morning the Dove and Dearne Canal at Wombwell was dragged for the body of a boy named John Harper, son of a miner living in School Street, Wombwell,

---

* This custom arose from the belief that the burning of the image would cause pain or death to the person whom it was intended to represent.

who has been missing since last night, and who is thought to have got into the water. He was seen with two other boys of about the same age fishing by the water's edge, and has not been heard of since. It may be that he has wandered off to Barnsley feast, for up to noon no sign has been discovered of him. In the endeavour to discover the body a singular old custom was invoked. A loaf of bread containing quicksilver was thrown upon the water, and the superstition is that it will suddenly stop and spin when it reaches the spot where the body lies. So firm is the belief, that sometimes sole dependence is placed upon this extraordinary method of ascertaining the whereabouts of the object sought for.

"Later in the afternoon it was discovered that the boy had wandered off to some relatives at Worsborough Dale, where he was found by his anxious parents, ignorant of the alarm his disappearance had caused."

To find out where a corpse lies in the water, take a piece of bread and throw it into the water. On the third day it will stand still over the place where the corpse is.

A little game played by children seems originally to have been a charm, but the purpose for which it was used is not now known. Two leaves are laid upon a table about two feet apart. Then a child puts his first fingers on the leaves, one upon each leaf, and says :

> Two little birds sat on a wall,
> One named Peter, the other named Paul ;
> Fly away, Peter, fly away, Paul.

After he has said the words "Fly away, Peter," he lifts up the right first finger, and throws the leaf over his right shoulder, and after he has said "Fly away, Paul," he lifts up the left first finger and throws the other leaf over his left shoulder. Then he puts the second finger of the right hand on the table and says, "Come back, Peter," and then the second finger of the left hand, saying, "Come back, Paul."

To see your future wife or husband in your dreams take a wedding-ring and draw a silk handkerchief through it. Then go backwards underneath the table, and so backwards to bed, and get into bed backwards.

The following charm is to be practised at midnight on St. Anne's Eve (July 26). A stool is set in the middle of a room, and a bowl of water put thereon. A string or piece of rope is then hung across the room. Seven unmarried girls, who must not speak till the ceremony is over, come in, and each hangs a smock on the line. Then each of the girls in turn drops a bay-leaf into the bowl of water, and sits down immediately opposite to the smock which she has hung up. Soon afterwards a young man will enter the room, take a bay-leaf from the bowl, and sprinkle the smock of the girl whom he intends to marry. He will marry her that year.

The following charm is practised on Midsummer Day:—A bucket of spring-water is set in the middle of a yard at midnight. If a girl looks therein at the hour of twelve she will see the face of the young man whom she is to marry. If she does not see it she will die an old maid.

If you rub the schoolmaster's cane with an onion it will split when he strikes you. Another way of splitting the cane is to lick the palm of your hand and lay a hair from your head across it.

Children sometimes link their little fingers together and wish something. By doing this it is supposed that the wish will be granted.

If two people begin accidentally to speak together on the same subject, or if they accidentally use the same word when they are beginning to speak, they should wish something, and the wish will be granted.

To keep evil spirits away get a bit of wood, make a cross of it, and nail it to your bedroom door.

When you first hear the cuckoo in the spring pluck up a handful of grass, and in it you will find a hair of the same colour as the hair of the man who will one day be your husband.

At Curbar, in Derbyshire, a young man was untrue to the girl who loved him. The girl thereupon took a live frog, stuck its body full of pins, and buried it. It is said that the young man suffered such severe pains in all his limbs after this that he came back to her an abject penitent. She then unearthed the frog, and removed the pins from its body. After this the pains left him, and he married her.*

In another instance related in East Yorkshire the girl "took a live frog, stuck it all over with pins, put it in a box, kept it shut up for a week, after which she looked in and found that the frog was dead. She kept it until it was consumed away to bones. Then she took out of the frog a small key-shaped bone, got into the company of the young man she wanted, fastened the bone to his coat, and said :

> I do not want to hurt this frog
> But my true lover's heart to turn,
> Wishing that he no rest may find
> Till he come to me and speak his mind.

After this he had a week's torture, as the frog had, and then he went to her and said he had had a queer sensation for a week, but he didn't know what it meant. 'However,' he said, 'I will marry thee, but I know we shall never be happy.' They were married and lived very uncomfortably together."

If your lover has forsaken you, and you want to bring him back to you, take a live pigeon, pluck out its heart, and stick pins therein. Put the heart under your pillow, and your lover will return to you.

When bread is baked it is usual to make a cross upon the flour in the pancheon when the bread is in the state called "sponge."

If butter does not come properly when you are churning tie a "withy of wiggin" (sprig of mountain ash) round your churn.

---

* My informant tells me that she knew these people well, that the young man's tortures caused a great stir in the neighbourhood, and that she thoroughly believes the story !

On All-hallows Eve Derbyshire girls put a sprig of rosemary and a crooked sixpence under their pillows in order that they may dream of their future husbands.

When you see a white horse, spit over your little finger, but do not look at the horse again, and you will find some money.

When you have a new coat do not put it on empty, but put something into the pocket for luck.

If you have lost anything, get a branch of yew and hold it out before you as you walk, when it will lead you straight to the place where the lost object is. When you have reached the object the branch will turn round in your hand.

. If you offer prayers near to salt they will always be answered. :

It is believed that the number seven is " the charm-number," and that it differs in some peculiar way from every other number.

On New Year's Day unmarried girls melt lead and pour it into a bucket of water. It then assumes various shapes, such as a hammer, and from this they divine the trades or occupations of their future husbands.

If your lover forsakes you buy two pennyworth of dragon's blood, and burn it on the fire. Whilst it is burning repeat these lines :

'Tis not this blood I wish to burn,
But [William's] heart I wish to turn ;
May he neither sleep nor rest
Till he has granted my request.

The same charm can be practised by throwing twelve pins into the fire at midnight and repeating similar lines.

If a woman wears nine pins inside her dress she can thereby torture her lover or husband. At Ridgeway, in Derbyshire, a woman was murdered by her husband, and after her death nine pins were found concealed in her dress.

When you are churning and the butter will not come, take a red-hot poker and touch each corner of the house with it. You will thereby drive the witch away.

Another way to make the butter come is to put a shilling into the churn.

When the first new moon of the year appears girls take a silk handkerchief and stand upon a hillock. They hold the handkerchief up to the moon, and looking through it say :

> New moon, new moon, I hail thee,
> I pray thee this night tell to me
> Who my true love shall be.

Then, having gone to bed, they see the images of their future husbands in their dreams.

To find out whether a person can keep a secret tickle the palm of his hand with your finger, and, looking him in the face, repeat these lines :

> Can you keep a secret,
> Can you keep it true ?
> Can you keep a secret
> All your life through ?
>
> Can you keep a secret ?
> I don't suppose you can.
> Don't laugh and don't cry
> Till it tickles in your hand.

If the person who is tickled laughs he cannot keep the secret.

On Shrove Tuesday girls toss up their shuttlecocks with the feathers downwards. They will have as many pancakes as the number of times they can toss the shuttlecock up in this way.

It is good for children to wear coral beads round their necks.

When a man is going out for a walk, and is undecided as to the way he shall go, he plants his walking-stick straight up on the ground, and then lets it fall. Whichever way the stick falls he will go.

Two persons take the "wishing-bone," or "lucky bone," of a fowl, and put it upon the oven to dry. When dry they seize it with their respective little fingers and break it. The one who gets the longest piece wishes something in secret, and his wish will come true. He will break the spell if he speaks before he has wished.

When children play at battledore and shuttlecock they say :

Apple tree, pear tree,
Pumpkin pie,
How many years
Before I die ?

They count the number of times they can keep the shuttle-cock up, which denotes the number of years they will live.

To find out whether your husband will have light hair or dark hair, take a table-knife with a white haft and spin it round on the table. If it stops with the blade towards you your husband will be a dark-haired man; if with the haft, he will be a light-haired man.

The following is a method of finding out how many years you will remain unmarried. Take a looking-glass and stand with your back to the full moon on a stone you have never stood on before. You will then see the moon reflected in the glass, and also a number of smaller moons. Count the number of smaller moons, and their sum will be the number of years you will have to remain unwed.

To find out whom you will marry, take a hard-boiled egg, remove the yolk, and fill it up with salt. Eat it fasting when you go to bed, and then you will dream of the person whom you will marry.

In Nottinghamshire on All-hallows Eve nuts are thrown into the fire, and wishes are expressed in secret. If the nut blazes the wish will be granted, but not if it " dies away." On this eve young men take a shallow tub, fill it with water, and put a sixpence at the bottom. They then duck their heads in, and the one who can pick it out with his teeth keeps it. An apple is also suspended from the ceiling of a room by a long string. The one who can catch it with his teeth is the lucky one. Apples are also roasted and the parings thrown over the left shoulder. Notice is taken of the shapes which the parings assume when they fall to the ground. Whatever letter a paring resembles will be the initial letter of the Christian name of the man or woman whom you will marry.

Let two girls take the bone of a fowl called the merry-thought and pull it asunder, and then let the one who gets the shortest piece put it in her pocket for three days. If the bone is brittle when taken out she will be married within a year.

The following charm is practised by girls in order that they may see the vision of their future husbands. A girl goes to a barn at midnight with a riddle or sieve, and opens both doors. She takes some corn, and " windows," or win-nows it, in the usual way, that night. She does the same on the two nights next following, when the spirit of her future husband appears.

On Christmas Eve unmarried girls lay a white sheet over a chair before the fire, and leave it there all night. In the morning if a spear is found reared against it the girl's husband will be a soldier; if a sickle, he will be a farmer, and so on.

To cross out a rainbow take two straws and lay one across the other. Then take four stones and lay one upon the end of each straw. Having done this the rainbow will go out. This charm is practised by children.

To dream of your future wife or husband walk backwards upstairs to bed for three successive Friday nights without speaking.

If a girl take a pea swad with nine peas in it, and hang it by a string over the outside of her house door, the first unmarried man who notices it will be her husband.

If a girl wishes to dream of her future husband let her go upstairs backwards on a Tuesday or a Friday night with a garter in her hands, saying these words as she ties it :-

> I tie my garter in two knots
> That I my beloved may see,
> Not in his best apparel,
> But in the clothes he wears every day.

If a girl walk backwards to a pear tree on Christmas Eve, and walk round it three times, she will see the spirit or image of the man who is to be her husband.

On Halloween people go out in the dark and pluck cabbage-stalks. If on this eve you scatter seeds or ashes down a lane, and a girl follows you in the direction in which you have gone, she will be your wife.

If you eat an apple at midnight upon All Halloween, and, without looking behind you, gaze into a mirror, you will see the face of your future husband or wife.

On New Year's Eve three unmarried girls may adopt the following plan in order to see the spirits of their future husbands. Let them go into a room which has two doors, and set the table with knives, forks, and plates for three guests, and let them wait in the room till twelve o'clock at midnight, at which hour exactly the spirits of their future husbands will come in at one door and go out at the other.*

Let a girl take the stone out of a plum, throw the stone in the fire, and say these lines:

> If he loves me crack and fly,
> If he hates me burn and die.

Then let her mention the name of her sweetheart. If he loves her the stone will crack and fly out of the fire. If he does not love her it will quietly burn to ashes.

Upon St. Mark's Eve, or upon Hallows Eve, at midnight let a girl go to a "four-lane-ends" or cross-way, taking some barley with her, then let her sprinkle the barley and say:

> Barley I sow, barley I trow,
> Let him who will my husband be
> Come after me and mow.

Then the future husband will come after her with a scythe

---

* The three guests are the three Parcae, or Fates. See Grimm's *Teut. Myth.* (trans. by Stallybrass), p. 1746.

and mow. Or the girl may sow hemp-seed in the garden and say :

> Hempseed I sow,
> Hempseed pray grow.

If it rain hard and you wish it to be fine, lay two straws across and the rain will cease. Apud comitatum Derbiensem duo pueri, secundum morem, ut dies serena sit, in forma crucis mingere solent, vel solebant.

On Midsummer Eve let a girl take a sprig of myrtle and lay it in her Prayer Book upon the words of the marriage service, "Wilt thou have this man to be thy wedded husband?" Then let her close the book, put it under her pillow, and sleep upon it. If her lover will marry her the myrtle will be gone in the morning, but if it remains in the book he will not marry her.

On Hallows Eve let a girl cross her shoes upon her bedroom floor in the shape of a T * and say these lines :

> I cross my shoes in the shape of a T,
> Hoping this night my true love to see,
> Not in his best or worst array,
> But in the clothes of every day.

Then let her get into bed backwards without speaking any more that night, when she will see her future husband in her dreams.

At a wedding let the bride pass small pieces of bride-cake through her wedding-ring, and give them to unmarried men and girls. If they put the pieces under their pillows for three nights, on the third night they will dream of their true lovers.

When you find two kernels inside a nut eat one of them, throw the other over your head, and wish something. After you have wished you must not speak to anybody until you can answer "Yes" to a question.

If you find an eyelash on one's cheek take it and put it upon the back of the hand. Then shut your eyes, blow three times, and guess at which blow it went off. Then wish

---

* The T represents the hammer or sign of the god Thor.

something, but do not speak to anybody until you can answer "Yes" to a question.

On Shrove Tuesday, or any other day when children are playing at battledore and shuttlecock, they say :

> Cuckoo, cherry tree,
> Come down and tell me
> How many years before I die.*

The number of times that you can keep the shuttlecock up is the number of years that you have to live.

There was a charm for a good harvest done by means of a peas-cod, which was plucked when the peas were just beginning to appear in the swad. Some lines were said in which the word "yield," as "give us a good yield," or some such phrase occurred. My informant remembers it very imperfectly, but thinks it was done by putting the thumbs alternately on the peas as the lines were recited.

To find out whether your sweetheart loves you or not, take a daisy and repeat the words "he loves me," "he loves me not," as you pluck each petal off. The last petal plucked will tell you the truth.

A ghost will vanish if you walk round it nine times.

The Devil hates salt and water. If you mix salt and water three times on a plate and sprinkle it upon anything, such as a dead man's coat, which is said to bring ill luck with it, and then make the sign of the cross thereon, the ill luck is taken away. This mixture of salt and water is called "holy lymph."†

To tell whether you are born to rule, clasp your hands together. If your right thumb be uppermost you will rule, but not otherwise.

To find out whether you will be rich or poor, take a single

---

* Pronounced *dee*. The question here put to the shuttlecock must once have been put to the cuckoo in spring, by those who believed in omens and auguries, in order to divine the number of years they had to live.

† Such were the words given to me. "Holy water is water wherein fine white salt hath been dissolved. Memorandum, there was no sacrifice without salt." Aubrey's *Remains of Gentilisme* (Folk-Lore Soc.), p. 121.

hair from your head and draw it between your wetted first finger and thumb. If it curls you will be rich, if not you will be poor.

There is a bone in a sheep's head, which is in shape somewhat like a cross, and is called "the lucky bone." In Derbyshire it is regarded as lucky to carry one of these bones in the pocket.

In Derbyshire divination was practised by means of a spiced wine, called sillibub (pronounced sillabub). Wine was poured into a bowl and then sweetened with sugar. A cow was milked into the bowl so as to make the mixture frothy. The mixture was then poured into wine-glasses, each containing a spoon. A ring was put into one of the glasses and a sixpence into another glass. The sillibub was drunk as the assembled guests were leaving, and this caused some excitement amongst the unmarried, for it was said that the one who got the ring would be married first, and the one who got the sixpence would die an old bachelor or an old maid.

If you want to prevent your beer from turning sour during a thunderstorm lay iron bars* across the barrels.

A man who was crossing a moor in East Yorkshire saw the *ignis fatuus*. Taking out his knife he planted it in the ground with the haft upwards. Next morning he found that the haft was quite eaten away.

Girls in Yorkshire used to take an ash leaf with even fronds, when they were fortunate enough to find one, and recite the lines:

> Even ash (esh) I pluck thee,
> In my bosom I put thee,
> Hoping this night my true love to see,
> Not in his vest, nor in his best,
> But in the clothes he wears every day.

---

* Supernatural beings had a great dislike for iron, as Mr. Hartland has shown in his *Science of Fairy Tales*. If the thunder was believed to be caused by a supernatural being this use of iron to prevent the beer from being injured by that being would be quite intelligible. Horse-shoes were used for the same reason, namely, as a protection against powers of evil, because they were made of iron.

In the evening the girl put the ash leaf under her pillow, and lay down to dream of her future husband.

To see the vision of your future husband, dip your smock into running water on St. Mark's Eve and hang it over a chair to dry. Then he will appear at midnight and turn the smock.

If you throw the "float," or air-gill, of a fish over the house-top it will become a silver spoon.

If you go out at midnight on St. Mark's Eve and pluck twelve sage leaves you will see your future husband.

A charm was practised in the East Riding by an egg and shovel put on the floor of a room at midnight, but I have not been able to get particulars.· A girl who practised this charm one night is said to have been so much scared by the appearance of the Devil that "she became converted and a member of the Wesleyan community."

VI.—LEECHCRAFT AND FOLK-MEDICINE.

To cure warts, take a bean swad and rub the warts therewith, when they will go away.

Another way to cure warts is to wet them each morning with a little spittle.

Another way is to twist a hair round the wart.

Another way is as follows: Take a green sprig of elder-wood and a penknife. Touch one of the warts with the point of the knife, and then cut a snip or notch in the sprig or stick of elder. When you have touched all the warts, one by one, with the point of the knife, and cut as many snips in the elder stick as there are warts on the patient's body, bury the stick in the ground. Then as the stick decays the warts will decay also.*

---

* A man who had thirty warts is said to have been treated in this way and cured !

Another way is to take a pea and bury it in a piece of lonely ground, or on a piece of land on which nobody treads. As the pea rots away the warts will disappear.

Another way is to rub them with an apple, or lick them with your tongue when you awake.

Another way is to take a black snail and stick it on a thorn in a hedge, or put it between two stones. As the snail's body perishes so will the warts perish.

Another way is to take oat-straws with knots in them, and having the same number of knots as there are warts on the patient's body. Count the warts on the afflicted person's body, and also the knots in the straws. Bury each straw separately, and as the straws decay in the ground the warts will die. You must do all this secretly.

Another way is to sell your warts for a small sum of money, when they will disappear.

Another way is to take as many cinders as you have warts, wrap them in paper, take a walk, and throw the cinders over your left shoulder, without looking back. When you have done this the warts will soon be gone.

Another way is to pretend to wash your hands in an empty bowl out of doors, keeping your face fixed on the full moon, for two succeeding nights. On the third night the warts will have gone.

A woman at Eckington, in Derbyshire, counted the warts on a man's hand and told him that the next time she saw him they would be gone.

Fuzz balls (*lycoperdon bovista*) are used to stop bleeding.

It is good for a dog to lick a wound.*

To keep the cramp away carry a potato in your pocket.

A cat's skin is a good remedy for toothache. You should keep a dried cat's skin and hold it to your cheek when your tooth aches.

To cure a cold, walk to a particular place one way and return another way.

* It is said of Lazarus the beggar that "the dogs came and licked his sores." *Luke* xvi. 21.

When children are cutting their teeth their mother should rub them with her wedding-ring.

To cure a child of the whooping cough, cut a lock from his hair and bury it in the ground.

If you put a puncheon of cold water under the bed on which a corpse lies the smell of the corpse will go down into the water.

If you lay a new-born child on its left side it will always be awkward.

A bed should point to the east and west, and not to the north and south. Restlessness is caused by placing the bed in the direction of north to south.

It is good for your health to follow the plough and smell the newly-ploughed earth.

If your finger-nails project in the middle you will die early.*

It is bad for one's health to fondle cats.

Salves and ointments should not be applied with the first finger, but with the middle or longest finger.

If a sudden shivering comes upon you death is running over your house.

If a child is put upon a bear's back at a bear-baiting he will be cured of the whooping cough.

A horse having fallen ill at Dore, near Sheffield, a man bled it, and then rubbed some of the blood into the horse's back, with the idea of strengthening that part.

At Dore, near Sheffield, the following wild herbs were "laid in," that is, hung up and dried, to be used for medicine, namely, meadow-sweet, mountain-flax, sanctuary, and wood-betony. Also the following garden herbs, namely, rosemary, hyssop, and herb-a-grass. They were plucked when in flower.

Poultices made of house-leek are good for "water-canker" and "blasts."

To cure the whooping cough, bore a hole into your door-

---

* Does this refer to the clubbed fingers of phthisis ?

post, put a live spider into the hole, and then stop the hole up. As the spider pines away the cough will die.

Another way is to put a spider into a nutshell, when the same thing will happen.

Still another way is to eat a fried mouse.

If a mother leaves her child, her breasts will be painful when the child cries.

To cure the ring-worm trace your finger round the child's face three times, and do this three times a day. On the third day the ring-worm will be cured.

If you have sore eyes poultice them with decayed apples.

The whooping cough can be cured by riding on a piebald horse.

To avoid cramp have a piece of cork in your bed.

To strengthen the spine rub yourself with grey snails.

If you put a worm into the right hand of a seventh son it will curl up, turn white, and die. This hand is known as "the poisonous hand."* A seventh son has the power to cure ring-worms by stroking them. He has also the power to cure warts by stroking them.

The seventh daughter of a real gipsy can tell fortunes.

If a man has a fever, lay a piece of feverfew in his bed, and he will be cured.

People sometimes sell their coughs and colds for a small sum of money.

If your tooth comes out put some salt on it and say :

> Good tooth, bad tooth,
> Pray God send me a good tooth.

Then throw the bad tooth into the fire, and a good tooth will come in its place. In the East Riding they eat sugar when a tooth is pulled out, and throw the tooth into the fire, saying:

> Fire, fire, here's a bone,
> Pray God send a tooth again.

* I shall not soon forget how an old man, now dead, assured me that on account of his being a seventh son a worm would curl up and die in his hand. He was very serious about this, and said that he had no doubt whatever of the fact ! The supposed possession of this power may be the origin of the surname Septimus. One never hears of Sextus as an English surname.

Some people sprinkle a little salt in water before they drink it.

If a child has the thrush, go and look for a frog. When you have found it, put it into the child's mouth, and then the thrush will be cured.

At Eyam, in Derbyshire, weakly children used to be anointed with May dew, which was collected in a sheet spread out on May eve. The dew was rubbed into the loins.

When children are stung by nettles they rub the injured part with a dock-leaf, and say :

> Dock, go in, nettle, go out ;
> Dock shall have a white frock,
> And nettle shall go without.

When a man is drowned his body always rises to the surface on the ninth day.

"One of the superstitions current at the present time in Yorkshire is a supposed cure for whooping-cough. When the patient is asleep cut off a bit of his, or her, hair, make an incision in the bark of a wiggin-tree, bury the hair in the crevice, and close up the opening. The patient will then recover. The woman who told me about it said she had tried the remedy with success." *

In Nottinghamshire they say that to prevent infection from fevers and other diseases you should burn an old shoe.†

When your hand tickles you should rub it on wood and not on leather. People say :

> If you rub it on wood
> It is sure to be good ;
> If you rub it on leather
> It is sure to gether.‡

* *Sheffield Daily Telegraph*, February 11, 1 92.

† The smell of burnt leather is very disagreeable. The Chinese believe that evil spirits dislike evil smells. Diseases were formerly regarded as the visitations of demons.

‡ To gather or fester.

VII.—OMENS: THINGS LUCKY AND UNLUCKY.

WHEN a calf is taken from the cowhouse to grass for the first time it must be taken with the tail foremost.

It is unlucky to have peacocks' feathers in your house.

If you dream of losing your teeth you will lose your best friend.

When you go to a new house poke the fire for luck.

Drop an eyelash and a wish will be granted.

The opal is an unlucky stone. If it cracks, evil is betokened.

It is unlucky to turn your bed on Friday or Sunday.

It is unlucky to walk under a ladder; if you do so you will be hanged.

It is unlucky to tell one's dreams before breakfast.

If you tell your dreams before breakfast they will come true.

If a new house is built a member of the family, and usually the head of the family, is almost sure to die.

If you dream of the dead you'll have trouble with the wick (living).

If a woman who has been delivered of a child goes visiting amongst her neighbours before she has been churched, she takes bad luck with her wherever she goes.

When you see the first lamb in spring, look which way its head is turned, for in that direction you will have to travel during the ensuing year.

If letters cross in the post they cross out love.

Parents should not keep locks of their children's hair if they wish them to live.

If you put cream in your tea before you put the sugar in you will cross your love.

If a man's fingers are long, and turned back at the ends, he cannot save money.

When gipsies come to your door, always buy something of them. Unless you do so they will wish that some evil may befall you, and their wish will be carried into effect. When gipsies first come into a village children sometimes say :

> Gipsy, gipsy, don't hurt me ;
> Heed yon girl behind yon tree.

If you spit on a gift, such as a piece of money, you will receive more.

It is unlucky to find a corn of wheat in a loaf of bread.

If a child's top teeth come before the teeth in the lower jaw he will die early.

If you can get a threepenny piece between the two front teeth in your top jaw you will be rich.

If you break a piece of glass you will not stop until you have broken three pieces, for by the odd number your luck will assert itself.

If you name a child after a brother or sister previously deceased it will die also.

If you have a mole under your left arm you will be wealthy. If you have a mole at the back of your neck you will be beautiful.

If you break a looking-glass you will have seven years' bad luck thereafter.

It is unlucky to remove from your house on Friday. It is said that :

> Friday flits have not long sits.

When people are unlucky at cards, or any other game, they should turn their chairs round ; that is, they should exchange places.

It is lucky for your first child to be a girl.

When you are playing at cards on a wooden table do not play across the grain of the wood.

In giving a name to a child it is unlucky to have three initials of the same letter, as S. S. S. or B. B. B. A child so named will die young.

It is unlucky to drink out of a jug or pitcher.

When you go out for a walk in the morning put your right foot out first.

When you see a baby for the first time you should give it something for luck.

If two people say the same thing at the same time they should lock their little fingers together and wish, and the wish will come true.

It is unlucky to meet an old woman when you go out in the morning.

If a collier meets a woman as he goes to his work in the early morning he regards it as a bad omen, and thinks that an accident will happen in the pit.

It is unlucky to meet a red-haired woman in the morning.

Stacks which are made on Sunday always get burnt down.

When the same figure appears in the year of Our Lord, as 1888, ill luck will come.

A man who cannot span his own wrist is born to be hanged.

It is unlucky to sing before breakfast. In the East Riding they say, " If you sing in the morning you will cry before bedtime."

If your toes are joined together by a web you will be lucky.*

Left-handed people are unlucky.

It is usual to prevent children from using their left hand, as, for instance, to pick a spoon up.

It is unlucky for a knife to be left across another knife on the table.

If your ears or cheeks burn someone is talking of you. People say :

> Right for love and left for spite,
> But either side is good at night.

A young woman should not look into a looking-glass too often, or she will see the Devil behind her.

If you laugh very heartily, or laugh till the tears come, you will have trouble afterwards.

When you are confirmed it is lucky to have the bishop's right hand on your head.

* This, I am told, is a *lusus naturae* which sometimes appears.

If you are wrapping up table-cloths, or other linen, or carpets, and the ends do not meet evenly, you will not be married that year.

A woman will never have good luck until she has worn her wedding-dress out.

It is unlucky to turn a spoon over in your mouth.

If pigeons sit on your window-sill death is at hand.

If you do not cut your bread evenly you will never be rich.

It is unlucky for a clock to stand opposite the fire.

If a baby girl is born with a mark between her eyes like a tiny spray of red currants she will be a beauty.

If a mother weighs a child before it is a year old the child will not live.

If a child has a blue vein across its nose it will die early.

It is unlucky to dream of new-laid eggs.

In the East Riding they say that if animals are fortunate in bearing young, for example, if sheep yield good " crops " of lambs in spring, the same spring will be lucky for women and babies.   It is said that 1874 " was a terrible year for farmers and husbands, for so many sheep and wives died."

When a farmer is about to sell a cow he must not milk her on the morning of sale.   If he milks her he will have no luck in selling her.

If you spill salt don't scrape it up, or you will have bad luck.   It is unlucky to spill salt, but you can cancel the ill luck by throwing some over your left shoulder, which is the side of the heart.

If thirteen dine at table together one of them is sure to die.   A sudden death often occurs afterwards.

It is said that :

> A whistling wife and a crowing hen
> Are neither good for God nor men.

In the East Riding they say that when a woman whistles the Devil rattles his chains.

If you have forgotten anything it is unlucky to turn back and fetch it.

When a man's cow gets into his neighbour's pasture she is said to be " unlucky."

If you find a hole or cavity in a piece of bread when you have cut into it, it is a sign of death.

If you meet a woman who squints it is bad luck ; if you meet a man who squints it is good luck.

To help another person to salt is to help him to sorrow.

It is unlucky to mend your clothes whilst you are wearing them.

If the first children of a family take the names of their parents they will die before the parents.

If you dream of pegging sheets out on a clothes-line you will soon have to prepare a shroud.

At Our Lord's last supper Judas Iscariot overturned the salt-cellar with his elbow, and that caused his bad luck.

To hear the rustle of paper is a sign of death.

It is lucky to carry the tip of a dried tongue in your pocket.

If you sit on a table you want to be married.

After you have worn red you will have to wear black, that is, there will be a death in your family.

If a man has once been rescued from drowning he is in no danger of being drowned afterwards.

It is lucky to have a horse-shoe, because its shape resembles the crown of thorns which Christ wore at his crucifixion, and because its shape also resembles the halo which surrounds a saint's head.*

If you point nine times at the moon you will not go to heaven.

If one stirs up the fire and it burns brightly another may say, " Your spark's bright to-night," meaning that your lover is in a good humour.

---

* This is not the true reason. The true reason is the dislike which in ancient belief supernatural beings had for anything made of iron.

If a shopkeeper gives credit to his customers on Monday morning he will have no luck that week.

Never carry anything into a house on your shoulders, especially a spade; if you do so you may have to carry a coffin in soon afterwards.

If you see a red spark in a candle a letter will come for you that day.

If a spark flies out of a candle the person towards whom it flies may expect a letter.

It is unlucky to rock an empty cradle.

If one borrows salt the borrower must not return salt to the lender. The lender must borrow from the borrower in return.

If your left ear burns people are speaking evil of you, but if your right ear burns they are speaking good.

Never lay a plan during a meal; if you do so the plan will not succeed.

If you hear three thumps in the house at night, or if you hear a willow-wand switch the door three times, it is a sign of death.

If a woman loses her garter in the street her lover will be unfaithful to her.

It is unlucky to take off your wedding-ring.

If seven girls in succession are born of a family the seventh will have ill luck. In some way it will differ materially from the others.

In the East Riding they say that if men sweep dust out of a house ill-luck will follow; women sweep dust up in the house for luck.

If you sweep dirt out of a house you will sweep all the money out.

When you sweep a house do not sweep the dust out at the door, or the good luck of the house will go with the dust.

If you bring dust downstairs after twelve o'clock you will soon have to carry a corpse down.

When beastlings are taken to a neighbour he should not

wash the pitcher out, or the cow and her calf will die. He should return the pitcher unwashed.

When a pig is killed, and fry is sent to a neighbour, the dish must not be washed out, or the pig will not take the salt.

If you stumble as you go upstairs there will be a wedding ✓ in the house.

It is unlucky to pass one on the stairs.

People who wipe on the same towel will go a-begging ✓ together.

If you wash in the water in which another person has washed you will quarrel with him. But you can prevent a quarrel by spitting in the water, or making the sign of the cross thereon.

If two people wipe their hands on the same towel they will quarrel.

It is unlucky to spin a knife round on the table.

If a knife falls a stranger is coming.

Two knives laid across one another on the table bring bad luck.

If three members of one family, being sisters and brother, or brothers and sister, marry on the same day, some person who attends the wedding will be sure to die.

If a cock crow on your doorstep a stranger is coming.

If one makes a present of a knife or a pair of scissors the ill luck thereby portended can be taken away by giving the donor a halfpenny.

It is unlucky to put a loaf on the table upside down, for the Devil is flying over the house when a loaf is the wrong way up.

If you cut both ends of a loaf off the Devil will fly over the house.

It is unlucky to take hold of a loaf or a piece of bread whilst another person is cutting it.

If a loaf of bread is placed on the table the wrong way upwards the bread-winner will fall ill.

When cattle are sold the seller must return a coin or a small sum for luck.

If the middle of your right hand itches somebody is about to bring you a present.

If your feet itch you are going to walk on strange ground.

When the sole of your foot itches you are going to tread on ground on which nobody has ever trodden before.

Crooked money brings good luck.

It is lucky to have a crooked sixpence in your purse.

It is lucky to put your stockings on with the wrong side outwards.

If your right eye itches you will have sorrow, if your left eye itches you will have joy; if your right hand itches you will pay away money, but if your left hand itches you will receive money; if your nose itches you are going to be kissed by a fool.

If you take flowers into a sick man's room you will make him much worse.

It is unlucky for four people to shake hands across.

If a young married woman can cut the finger-nails of her right hand with her left hand she will rule her husband.

When you comb your head and throw hair into the fire take notice whether the hair blazes or "crozzils up." If it blazes you will live long. If it "crozzils up" you will die soon.

If your apron falls off somebody is thinking about you.

If you splash yourself or wet yourself very much when you wash clothes you will have a drunken husband.

It is unlucky to put a lantern on the table, and people say :

> A lantern on the table
> Is death in the stable.

To dream of a wedding is a sign of a funeral, and to dream of a funeral is a sign of a wedding.

To dream of a cat is a sign that you have a very deceitful friend.

It is unlucky to give a pin away ; you should only lend.

If in talking you make rime wish something and your wish will be granted.

If any article of household use falls from a wall the owner of that article will die.

A wedding-ring must not be used twice; for instance, a daughter must not wear her mother's wedding-ring:

> For a twice-used ring
> Is a fatal thing;
> Her griefs who wore it are partaken,
> Beware that fatal ring.

If your left ear burns somebody is abusing you. You should make the sign of the cross thereon three times, and then the slanderer will bite his own tongue.

Those who have much hair on their arms are sure to be rich.

Let a spoon fall and a fool will come to see you.

If a fire burns hollow, or divides itself into two parts, it is a sign of a parting.

It is a sign of death if the sexton accidentally rings the passing-bell.

At Eyam, in Derbyshire, it is said that if the sound of the passing-bell be very clear there will soon be another death in the village.

When a gaseous piece of coal makes a spluttering noise it is a sign of a row; you should give it a vigorous stir.

If a girl's hair fall down, or if her shoe-lace becomes untied, her lover is thinking of her.

A blacksmith in Sheffield would not work again on any day, if, when he threw his hammer down, it fell with the handle standing upwards.

It is unlucky to put boots or shoes on the table.

If you wish something when you see a piebald horse you will obtain your wish.

It is unlucky to count your teeth.

It is said that:

> If you toast on a knife
> You'll be poor all your life.

Bread must not be toasted on a knife.

It is unlucky not to go to a funeral when you are invited.

It is unlucky to sharpen a knife after sunset.

If the joints of a corpse are loose another death in the family will follow shortly. In East Yorkshire the women who prepare the corpse for burial say that if it is "leth-waite," or limp, there will soon be another death in the family.

To dream of a death for three nights in succession is a sure sign that a death is about to happen in your family.

If a child dies, and its neck does not become stiff shortly after death, there will soon be another death in the family.

If plants or flowers that are given to you keep fresh for a long time the giver is true to you; if they die soon he is false.

If a child's nails are cut before it is twelve months old it will be a thief.

If you let your stick fall you will be sure to meet a friend immediately afterwards.

If a girl strides over a besom-handle she will be a mother before she is a wife. If an unmarried woman has a child people say " She's jumped o'er t' besom," or " She jumped o'er t' besom before she went to t' church." Mothers used to be particularly anxious that their daughters should not stride over a broom, and mischievous boys have been known to leave brooms on door-steps, and such like places, so that girls might accidentally stride over them.*

If you see a white horse, spit on your little finger, and you will be lucky all day.

It is unlucky to let a child look into a mirror before it can walk.

If you put a widow's bonnet on you will become a widow yourself.

Never buy black pins unless you are in mourning.

---

* In Sheffield a woman of loose habits is called a *beesom*, or *besom*. See the word in my *Sheffield Glossary.* Compare the superstitions about witches and their stick and broom riding. Grimm's *Teut. Myth.*, p. 1083.

If you put a black pin into a piece of work you will never finish it.

If you accidentally put your clothes on inside outwards you will have something given to you.

VIII.—DAYS AND SEASONS.

In Derbyshire "wassil" cakes are made on New Year's Day. They are composed of flour, milk, and the first egg which a goose has laid. The cake is the same as that which is known as "speechless cake."

In Nottinghamshire the wassail bowl goes round on Christmas Eve. First the Christmas cake is broken up and put into the bowl. Then hot ale is poured over the cake, and all eat together.

Near Penistone, in South Yorkshire, a large apple-pie was made on Christmas Eve, and a posset-pot was filled with posset, made of ale and milk mixed together. A large spoon was put into the posset-pot, which was placed in the middle of the kitchen table. Round this table sat the master of the house and all his household. The posset-pot was passed from one to another round the table; as soon as one had drunk enough it was passed on to the next, all the household taking a "sup" one by one, and using the same large spoon. Then the apple-pie was passed round in the same manner.

Ale posset must be the last thing that you drink on Christmas Eve, and frummity the first thing that you eat on Christmas morning.

At Penistone, when the yule log was burnt on Christmas Eve, the fire was not allowed to go out during the night. In the morning, whatever burning ashes were left in the grate were carefully collected and taken down into the cellar, when they were put under the "milk benk."* These ashes were

* The stone bench on which the pancheons or vessels of milk stood.

supposed to "keep the witch away" during the following year, and bring good luck to the house. They were kept for years, forming a great pile in the cellar, and were not allowed to be taken away.

In Derbyshire it is said that if the yule log is not burnt away on Christmas Eve the ashes or embers must on no account be taken out of the house. No fire must on any account be taken out of the house between Christmas Eve and New Year's Eve.

In Nottinghamshire it is said that there must always be a portion of last year's yule log left in the house to be burnt upon the next Christmas Eve. A bit of last year's log must first be put into the fireplace and burnt. When that has been done the fresh log must be put on the fire and be allowed to burn for a little while. It must then be taken off and burnt a little every night until New Year's Eve. On New Year's Eve the log must be put on the fire, but it must not be all burnt away. What is left must be kept in the house until next Christmas Eve.* It is believed that the observance of this custom will "keep the witch away."

If you meet with a good log of wood you should preserve it for the Christmas fire.

In the East Riding the yule cake, which was made in the evening a day or two before Christmas Day, was eaten on Christmas Eve. It was made of flour, barm, large cooking raisins, currants, lemon-peel, and nutmeg, and was about as large as a big dinner-plate, and about three inches thick. It was crossed by a network of pastry in small squares. Before the eating of the yule cake began, a yule log was put on all the fires in the house except the fires in the bedrooms. In some families a loving-cup went round, of which every person at table took about a wine-glass full. The assembled company drank at the same time standing on chairs. Then the health of the oldest member of the family was proposed.

* As to the sacred fire which was never allowed to go out, see Mr. Gomme's *Folk-Lore Relics of Early Village Life*, p. 96. The Christmas fire was a piece of magic whereby it was hoped to ensure warmth during the coming year.

In the East Riding the peasantry ate nuts on Christmas Eve, and if the moon was full they went out into the open air and said :

> Yull, yull, yull, my belly's full,
> Cracking nuts and crying yull, yull, yull.

It is unlucky to continue the knitting of a stocking into the new year. The stocking should be finished before the year closes, and the needle taken out. The needle must not be allowed to remain in the stocking until the beginning of the new year.

As the old year is passing away and the new year coming in cattle fall on their knees.

Whatever work you are doing when the new year comes in you will do a great deal of the same work during that year.

If you refuse a mince-pie at Christmas you will be unlucky during the following year. As many mince-pies as you eat between Christmas Day and the new year so many happy months will you have.

It is unlucky to come into your house with empty hands on New Year's morning.

A candle or lamp should be left burning all night on Christmas Eve. Unless this is done there will be a death in the house. It was usual for the grocers in Yorkshire to present their customers with candles at Christmas. They were made for the purpose, and were burnt on Christmas Eve. Usually one very large candle was given; sometimes two smaller ones. The custom is now disused, and the grocers send their advertising almanacks instead.

In some parts of Yorkshire master-joiners sent their apprentices round at Christmas time with yule logs, or yule clogs, as presents to their customers.

In the East Riding the following custom was observed. At the dawn of Christmas Day the head of the family let in a boy called the "lucky bird," who brought a sprig of ever-greens. He was presented with a sixpence, something to eat and something to drink; the repast usually consisting of yule cake and cheese, with mead or sweet home-made wine. The boy was not always dark-haired, as in the West Riding. After the "lucky bird" had been, every member of the family went out of the house unwashed (not even the hands were allowed to be washed) and carried a sprig of evergreen into the house. Up to twelve o'clock at noon boys who sang carols were admitted. On this day no woman, not even the nearest relation, was allowed to enter the house, or it brought ill luck, and only men and boys received gifts. On New Year's Day the "lucky bird" came again and received the usual present. Then the boys of the family received presents, and after them the girls.

On Christmas Eve, or the morning of Christmas Day, you should give a sheaf of oats to every horse, cow, or other beast about your farmhouse.

If a dog howls on Christmas Eve he will go mad in the following year.

Evergreens brought into the house before Christmas should not be taken out of the house until Christmas is over, or until Twelfth Day.

On the last day of the old year a great gust of wind blows across the face of the earth, and all the earth is then changed.

On New Year's Eve one should go out before midnight and bring a piece of coal, a broom, a shovel, or other article into the house. This should be done just as the old year is passing away and the new year coming in. A piece of money should also be put into the spout for luck, and taken into the house just when the new year is coming in.

If a woman goes out of the house on Christmas Eve she must return before midnight.

The first person who comes into a house on New Year's morning must have black hair. Sometimes boys with dark hair are picked for the purpose of being the first to enter the house on New Year's morning. It is unlucky for a light-haired or a red-haired man to "let in" Christmas. In the north of Derbyshire, and also in Sheffield, it is a very common practice to ask some dark-haired man to come into the house on the morning of Christmas Day before any other person has entered. The same man will often "let in" Christmas for a number of families, calling at their houses early in the morning. He usually walks in at the front door and goes out at the back door. In many houses the custom is very strictly maintained.

If the sun shines brightly on your apple trees on the morning of Christmas Day you will have a good crop of apples next year.

It is said in South Yorkshire that as Christmas draws near ghosts or spirits become more powerful.* Many people have the greatest objection to being left alone on Christmas Eve.

The following carol is sung on Christmas Day and New Year's Day in the neighbourhood of Sheffield. It is called:

JOLLY WESSEL BOUGH (BOO).

Girls. Our jolly wessel,
    Love and joy come to you,
    And to our wessel bough (boo);
    Pray God send you
    A happy new year,
    A new year, a new year.
    We've been a while a-wandering
    Amongst the leaves and greaves,†
    And now we come a-wesseling,
    So plainly to be seen.
Boys. God bless the master of this house,
    And the mistress also,
    Likewise the little children
    That round the table go.
    I wish you a merry Christmas
    And a happy new year,
    A pocket full of money,
    And a cellar full of beer,

* "As the night lengthens, and the day shortens, the ghosts gain strength, and reach their highest at Yule time."—Cleasby and Vigfusson's *Icelandic Dict. s.v.* jól, p. 326.

† Old English *græfe*, a greave, or grove. The version here printed was written down by me on Christmas Day, 1890.

A apple and a pear,
A plum and a cherry,
And a sup o' good ale
To make a man merry.
We've got a little purse
Made of ratchet leather * skin :
We want a little of your money
To line it well within.

At Eckington, in Derbyshire, a village about eight miles
from Sheffield, the children carry a doll in a box when they
go round singing this carol. In Nottinghamshire an old
woman used to go round from house to house with a doll in a
cradle. She used to sing a number of verses, which my
informant has forgotten. As she was leaving a house she
sang :

And now my song is ended,
I cannot sing no more.
1 thank you for t' civility
I have received here ;
I wish you a merry Christmas,
And a happy new year.

In Eckington another hymn or carol† is sung by children on
Christmas Eve, the words and tune being as follows :

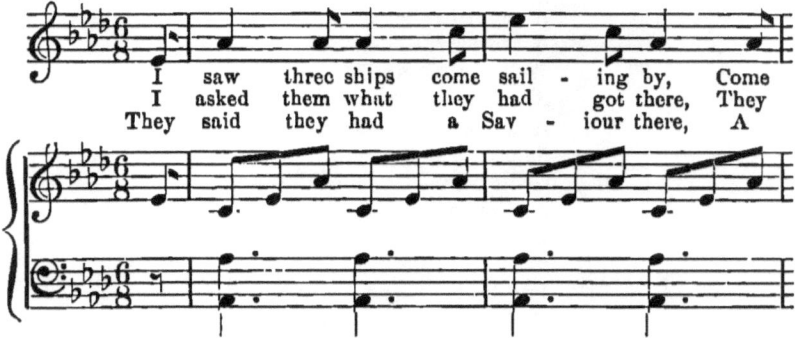

I   saw   three ships   come sail - ing by,   Come
I   asked   them what   they had   got there,   They
They said   they had   a Sav - iour there,   A

* Some say " stretching leather." *Ratch*, to stretch, occurs in the dialect.
† It seems probable that the singer of this carol formerly carried a box
containing the figure of a child. This is called the " bessel cup " in North
Yorkshire, or the " milly box." (Henderson's *Folk-Lore*, 1879, pp. 65 and 66.)
The boy in the ship will remind the reader of the boy Scef, or Sceaf, who, as
the legend goes, came in a ship to Scedeland or Scandia. (Rydberg's *Teut. Myth.*,
p. 87.) I published this hymn with some comments in the *Gentleman's Magazine*,
July, 1890.

sail - ing by, come sail - ing by, I saw three ships come
had got there, they had got there, I asked them what they
Sav - iour there, a Sav - iour there, They said they had a

sail - ing by, At Christ - mas day in the morn - ing.
had got there At Christ - mas day in the morn - ing.
Sav - iour there At Christ - mas day in the morn - ing.

They washed his head in a golden bowl,
In a golden bowl, in a golden bowl,
They washed his head in a golden bowl
At Christmas day in the morning.

They wiped his head with a diaper towel,
With a diaper towel, with a diaper towel,
They wiped his head with a diaper towel
At Christmas day in the morning.

They combed his hair with an ivory comb,
With an ivory comb, with an ivory comb,
They combed his hair with an ivory comb
At Christmas day in the morning.

And all the bells in heaven did ring,
Heaven did ring, heaven did ring,
To think that Christ was born a king
At Christmas day in the morning.

About Dronfield, in Derbyshire, they sing at Christmas the carol beginning :

> The first good joy that Mary had it was the joy of one
> To see her own son Jesus suck at her breast-bone;
>   It brings tidings of comfort and joy.*

In the East Riding girls, who were called " vessel cups," came to the door at Martinmas time, or the end of November. They carried a deep box in which were two dolls of different sizes, and sang the carol :

> God arest (*sic*) you merry Christians,
> Let nothing you dismay,
> Remember Christ our Saviour
> Was born on Christmas Day.

In the East Riding carol-singers were called " wakes."

In that part of Yorkshire women went about on St. Thomas's Eve asking for gifts of wheat or money for their frummity on Christmas Eve. Church bells were rung at seven on that eve, and then the frummity was put on the fire.

If you hang clothes out to dry on Old Christmas Day (January 12) you will be laid in your grave in some of those clothes before the year is out.

On Twelfth Day the bakers of Sheffield used to bake immense cakes called " twelfth cakes." On one occasion an unusually big one was made by a Mr. Walker, whose shop was in High Street. It was baked in sections, and was paid for by subscription. The *Sheffield Iris* mentions a colossal Christmas pie, prepared for a convivial party by Mr. Roberts

---

* The words of the carol are the same as those given in Brand's *Popular Antiquities*, ed. 1849, i. 454. In singing the carol the last line of each stanza is repeated several times. The " vessel cup," is not carried about in Dronfield, but it is carried about in the village of Handsworth, near Sheffield. Taking the whole evidence together, it seems to me that the " box," " milly box," " bessel cup," or " vessel cup," represents the image of a vessel or ship in which an effigy of the boy Sceaf (afterwards changed to Jesus) was carried about as a representation of the birth of the year. *Vessel*, or *fessel*, in the sense of ship, is at least as old as Chaucer's time. The idea seems to have been that the New Year, like a child, came over the sea in a ship.

in Fargate, which consisted of 56 lb. of flour, 30 rabbits, 43 lb. of pork, 12 lb. of veal, and 20 lb. of butter, pepper, &c. The weight was 13 stone 13 lb.*

On Candlemas Day Christmas decorations should be burnt. Old women in Nottinghamshire call it Blaze Day.

It is said in Derbyshire that birds of all kinds pair on Valentine's Day.

At Ompton, in Nottinghamshire, the young men and women used to go round begging for pennies on Valentine's Day, and men servants had half a day's holiday.

A man will marry the first girl that he meets on Valentine's morning, and a girl will marry the first man that she meets on that morning.

It is unlucky not to be standing on grass when you first hear the cuckoo; you ought not to be standing on a stone. At Dore, near Sheffield, scythe-grinders did not begin their business until the cuckoo's voice had been heard.

When you first hear the cuckoo, run as fast as you can until you are tired. Then take off your shoe, and in it you will find a lock of your lover's hair.

In South Yorkshire a custom called "footing the cuckoo" is observed. The following extract from the *Sheffield Daily Telegraph* of June 5, 1889, will describe the ceremonies:

"Thomas Wommersley, moulder, Burncross, and John Rogers, moulder, Chapeltown, were summoned for having been drunk and disorderly at Chapeltown, on the 22nd of last month. It was stated that the men with others on the day in question were observing the custom of the country known as "footing the cuckoo." On the day when the note of the cuckoo is first heard in the vicinity, the men get as many gallons of beer as they possibly can, take it to Norfolk Woods, consume it, and generally make merry. On the present occasion the defendants had procured twenty-one gallons, which they had with others consumed, and when police-constable Ellerby found them they were wheeling the

* *Gentleman's Magazine*, 1824, Part ii. p. 588.

empty barrels home from the woods, the effects of the beer being clearly discernible in the behaviour of the men. They were each find 16s. 6d., including costs."

At Austwick, near Settle, in the West Riding, the villagers had noticed that when the cuckoo was about the weather was generally fine. So they thought that if they could always keep the cuckoo they would always have fine weather. One season when it rained very hard, and they could not get their hay in, instructions were given that when a cuckoo had been seen in one of the small "plantins," or woods, in the neighbourhood the village should be warned. So when the cuckoo appeared warning was given, and the morning after the warning all the villagers turned out to build a wall round the wood where the cuckoo was. The work was heavy, but by dinner-time they had got the wall up to the height of six or seven feet. But whilst they were eating their dinners the cuckoo, to the great astonishment of all, was seen to fly from the trees towards the wall, and just managed to get over the top. And it was always said that if they had only built the wall one round of stones higher the bird could never have got out.

Season after season a farmer in this village had been very unlucky with his crops. He cut his grass at the usual time, and one day the sun dried it, and another day the rain came and wet it. So he thought the best thing would be to take the grass into the barn as soon as it was cut, and then bring the sunshine into the barn. So one day they found him busy with his cart. First he took the cart out into the sunshine, and let the sun shine on it for a few minutes, and then he began to tie the sunshine on with ropes. After he had done this he led the horses and cart into the barn, took the rope off the cart, and kicked the sunshine on to the grass.

There was a deep, dark pool at Austwick, whose banks were a favourite resort of men and boys. One day a man fell into the pool, and did not come up again, but presently a number of bubbles came up, making a strange noise, which seemed to the rest to take the form of words, and to say,

" T' b—b—b—best 's at t' b—b—bottom." So they all
jumped in one after another, to see what this good thing
was. And hence comes the local proverb " T' best 's at t'
bottom, as the Astic * carles say."

Many centuries ago there was only one knife in the village,
and it, for the sake of convenience, was kept in a large
hollow tree in or near the village. If anybody wanted the
knife, and it was not there, he let all the villagers know by
shouting " T' whittle † to t' tree, t' whittle to t' tree," and
then the man who had the knife had to produce it, or account
for its absence. One day, a number of men who were going
to cut ling on the fells, borrowed the whittle for that purpose.
As they intended to cut ling on the following day, they
thought it was no use taking the whittle home again if they
could find a safe place to put it in. After some search they
found a large dark patch on the moor, which could be seen
from a long distance. And so they put the whittle in one
corner of the patch, and covered it over with a lump of ling.
Next morning not a trace of the dark patch could be found,
and the whittle was irretrievably lost. Long afterwards they
found that they had laid the whittle in the corner of a shadow
caused by a passing cloud.

Other tales are told about these " Astic " men, all tending
to show that they were witless. The point in one of these
stories is that it is easier to let a bull go through a gateway
than to lift him over the gate.

If you have no money when you first hear the cuckoo you
will have poor luck that year.

On a certain day ‡ in the year women sweep the dirt from
their doorsteps in order to keep fleas away from the house
that year.

Servants must not begin their service on a Friday or
Saturday. If they do so they will quarrel with their masters
or mistresses.

---

* The local pronunciation of Austwick
† Knife.
‡ I was not told on what day.

I

If you cut your hair on either Thursday, Friday, or Saturday you will be poor all your life.

It is unlucky to go a-fishing on a Friday.

Those who wash on Friday wash for need; those who wash on Saturday are sluts indeed.

It is unlucky to cut your hair on Good Friday.

If clothes are washed and hung out to dry on Good Friday they will be found sprinkled with blood.

You must never yoke or work a horse on Good Friday.

Those who are born on Good Friday will know a murderer when they see one.

You must not begin a journey, or any fresh work, on a Friday.

Your finger-nails, or toe-nails, must on no account be cut on Friday or Sunday.　The following lines thereon are said:

> Monday for health,
> Tuesday for wealth,
> Wednesday for news,
> Thursday new shoes,
> Friday for sorrow,
> Saturday see your sweetheart to-morrow,
> If you cut them on Sunday you cut them for evil,
> And all the week through you will sup with the Devil.

If children swing on Sunday the Devil will either come or rattle his chains.

People say to children:

> You must not play on Sunday
> Because it is a sin;
> But you may play on Monday
> Till Sunday comes again.

It is unlucky to turn beds over on Sunday.

If you gather nuts on Sunday the Devil will fetch you. If you gather nuts on that day the Devil will put three nuts on the tree for every nut that you pull off.

On Collop Monday, which is the day before Shrove Tuesday, poor people in Derbyshire used to go to their richer neighbours to beg a collop of bacon to make fat for frying pancakes on the following day. At Dronfield Grammar School a bell called "the Pancake Bell" used to be rung on the morning of Shrove Tuesday for half an hour, after which the boys had holiday. Children in this parish have been seen going towards the church with large open baskets to catch the pancakes which, it is said, are thrown over the church steeple on that day. At Eyam, on the morning of Shrove Tuesday, the boys in the village rose as early as one or two o'clock, blew cow-horns,* rattled old cans, and made a great uproar. The boy who remained longest in bed on the morning of that day was called "the bed churn."

In the East Riding a girl who could not turn a pancake on Shrove Tuesday was not considered eligible for marriage.

You must not marry during the season of Lent.

Easter Monday is known in North Derbyshire as "Unlousing Day," † or "Lousing Day." On this day the men heaved, lifted, and kissed the girls. An old woman said that when she was in service near Wormhill, sixty years ago, four or five of the men-servants in the house did their utmost to fix her in a chair to be lifted and kissed. At Hathersage a young man was fined for kissing a young woman on this day. The practice of *unlousing* was known at Baslow and at Bamford. At Bradwell, if a young man meets a young woman on this day he steals a kiss and *unlouses* her. In that village the day is known as "Lousing Day."

On Easter Sunday it was the custom at Bradwell, in Derbyshire, for children to drop pins into the various wells in the town. It was said that a fairy presided over each well, and knew whether a child had deposited a pin in her well or not. On the following Monday every child carried a

---

* Aubrey in his *Remaines of Gentilisme*, ed. by Britten, 1881, p. 18, says that amongst the May customs "at Oxford the boyes doe blow cows horns and hollow caxes all night."

† To *unlouse* is to release, or set free. It would appear that kissing, as well as marrying, was considered unlawful during Lent, the sexes being set free (unloused) to marry at Easter. In South Yorkshire marriages are still very frequent on Easter Monday.

bottle all day long, which was filled with sweetmeats, a large quantity of sweetmeats being sold in the village on that day. The younger children had their bottles tied round their necks. It was said that the bottles of those children who had not dropped a pin into one of the wells would break, tho fairy of the well being the protector of the bottle. There were four or five wells in the town, one of them being in a place called "Daniel's Garden." In the East Riding children carried bottles on Easter Monday filled with clear water, into which Spanish juice was dropped. At Bradwell the children went round to every house begging for a present of sugar.*

In the East Riding children visited their parents on Easter Sunday, and the customary dinner was veal pie. In some parts Mid-Lent Sunday was called "Go-a-Mothering Sunday."

In Derbyshire the last night in April is called "Mischief Night." Then boys and young men throw bricks down chimneys, pull gates off their hinges, and do all sorts of wanton mischief. But if you hang a brush, shovel, or broom outside your house the mischief-makers will pass by the house and do no harm.

On Holy Thursday no bird will carry a feather to its nest. Barkers and pillers, that is, men who strip the bark from trees, will not climb trees on this day. If you hang clothes out on this day there will be a death in your family before the end of the year.

It is said that:

> If you plant a slip in May
> It will ne'er decay.

Children born in the month of May require great care in bringing up, for "May chickens come cheeping."

In the East Riding of Yorkshire the Martinmas Sunday dinner consisted of a roast goose.

In the East and West Ridings school children call Shrove

---

* An article entitled "Sugar-Cupping in the Peak of Derbyshire," in Hone's *Every-day Book*, 1827, p. 451, gives a very poor account of this custom.

Tuesday "Ball Day." On this day every child has a half-holiday and a new ball, which is made of four pieces of coloured leather sewn together and filled with sawdust. Everybody catches one of these balls when it is thrown up, and it is said that if you do not "kep," or catch, a ball before noon on this day you will be ill all through the ensuing harvest.

IX.—WEATHER LORE.

In Nottinghamshire it is said that :

> If Candlemas Day be fine and clear
> We shall have winter all the year.

A fine autumn is known as " St. Luke's summer." It is said that :

> If the oak precedes the ash
> Then we may expect a splash ;
> But if the ash precedes the oak
> Then we may expect a soak.

If it be fine on Easter morning it will be fine at the following harvest time. The saying is " A fine Easter, a fine harvest."

If it freezes for three whole days together rain will follow.

When the " mark " of a cat's eye broadens there will be rain.

If it rains on Friday it will rain on Sunday.

If the northern lights appear at harvest time there will be thunder.

On a very bright night, when "a white streak of stars " is seen in the sky, you can tell by the direction which the streak takes whether the weather will be wet or fine on the following day. If the direction of the streak is from east to

west it will rain next day; if from north to south it will be
fine.

If the new moon is "on its back," or "has its back downwards," the following month will be stormy.

It is said that:

> A red sky at night
> Is the shepherds' delight;
> A red sky in the morning
> Gives the shepherds warning.

Rainbows are keenly watched in the East Riding.

If your cat lies with her back to the fire it is going to rain.

In the East Riding children say:

> Rain, rain, go away,
> Come again another day;
> Rain, rain, come down and pour,
> Then you'll only last an hour.

In Derbyshire it is said that the weather in February is
not as it ought to be unless one can see a white horse at a
distance of a mile.

In Yorkshire people will not eat or do any kind of work
during a thunderstorm.

In the East Riding they say that if women frisk and run
about it is a sure sign of rain.

In Derbyshire farmers used to carry a candle down the
garden on All Hallows' Een, to see which way the wind
blew. As the wind blew that night such would be the pre-
vailing wind for the next three months.

Yorkshire farmers closely watch the different appearances
of the clouds. They imagine that one shape of cloud resembles Noah's Ark, and when they see it they say, "The
ark is up." If the "ark" points to the south-east, or
towards the Humber, they say that fine weather will follow.
When different strata of clouds appear before a storm
the various shapes of the lower strata are called "wild
horses," and one hears people say, "Oh, it will be a storm;

the wild horses are out." They call a sky which is flecked with many small clouds a " mackerel sky," and say that :

> A mackerel sky
> Is never long dry.

If black snails cross your path rain is certain.

X.—BIRTH, BAPTISM, MARRIAGE, DEATH, AND BURIAL.

CHILDREN who are born at twelve o'clock at midnight have the power, in after life, to see spirits. They have also the power to hear the Gabriel hounds. Children who are born at that hour are also gifted.

Children who are born during the " chime hours " of a parish church clock, that is, at the hours when musical tunes are chimed, have the power to see spirits.

During the first month of its life a baby sees in dreams the events of its whole future life.

The day on which a child is born influences its whole future life. It is said that :

> Monday's child is fair of face,
> Tuesday's child is full of grace,
> Wednesday's child is loving and giving,
> Thursday's child works hard for a living,
> Friday's child is full of woe,
> Saturday's child has a journey to go ;
> But the child that is born on the Sabbath Day
> Is merry and happy, and wise and gay.

On the birth of a child the father and his friends drink to its health, and this they call "washing baby's head." In the East Riding they say " wetting baby's head."

At Crookes, near Sheffield, a cloak with a hood, called a christening hood, was kept by one Sarah Stead, who let it out to hire to poor parents in the village who had a child to baptize.   For this she received a small sum, such as three-pence or fourpence.

In the East Riding they say that if a child screams at its christening it is resisting Satan.

It is unlucky for children to cry whilst they are being baptized.

A child which dies before it is christened will not go to heaven.

Children who are ill-tempered before baptism will be good-tempered after they have been baptized.   They will also sleep better and thrive better.   In this respect baptism acts as a charm.

Some people carry a plate of salt into the church at baptism.*   They say that a child which is baptized near salt will be sure to go to heaven when it dies.

Great care is taken of the veil, or caul, which sometimes surrounds a child's head when born.   The child which is so born can tell by means of the caul when trouble or when good fortune is coming upon him.   When trouble is coming the caul will be soft and flabby, but things will prosper so long as it remains dry, hard, and stiff.

Children who are still-born must be buried before sunrise, or in the night, or they will not go to heaven.   Burial of such children by night is very common in Derbyshire.   No funeral service is read.

For marriage there are lucky and unlucky days, and the following lines are said:

> Monday for health,
> Tuesday for wealth,
> Wednesday the best day of all,
> Thursday losses,
> Friday crosses,
> Saturday no luck at all.

---

* Amongst the Norsemen it was usual to put salt into the mouth at baptism. In Iceland a cross-shaped salt-cellar was used in church at baptism. Cleasby and Vigfusson's *Dict.*, pp. 195, 510. The object was to keep the witch away.

It is unlucky to get married in May. When a woman marries she should wear on her wedding-day:

> Something old, something new,
> Something borrowed, something blue.

Some say that these things should be made up into one piece.

It is unlucky to be dressed in green at a wedding.

It is unlucky to dress in your wedding-clothes before the wedding-day.

Be a bridesmaid thrice and you will never become a bride.

If you learn the marriage service you will never have to say it.

If you touch or rub against the bridegroom at a wedding you will soon be married.

If people marry on Friday they will "lead a cat-and-dog life," that is, they will quarrel.

If a younger brother or sister marries before his or her elder brother or sister, such elder brother or sister should dance on his or her stocking feet on the wedding-day.

As a woman's wedding-ring wears so do her troubles wear.

When a woman marries she must change the initial letters of her surname, or she will marry for worse and not for better.

At weddings it is usual to throw an old shoe or two after the bridegroom and bride as they are leaving the bride's house, and also to scatter some rice upon them.

In Derbyshire it is customary to pour a kettleful of boiling water over the doorstep just as the bride leaves the house on her way to church. It is said that before the water dries up another wedding will be arranged in the house. In some cases the water is poured over the doorstep "after the bride and groom have entered," it being said that the next girl who enters will become a bride, provided that her dress is wetted. This generally happens to be the first bridesmaid.

On the wedding-day the bride must always cut the cake

herself, or ill luck will happen. In the East Riding, after
the wedding is over and the bridal party are leaving the
house, an attendant hands a plate of bride-cake to the bridegroom, who throws it over the bride's head, and the more
pieces it is broken into the more good luck the bride and
bridegroom will have.

Races for ribbons were common in Yorkshire at weddings.
These races were run in front of the bride's house. The first
two ribbons were called "the bride's garters," and he who
won the race had a right to kiss the bride. These ribbons
were generally white, and three or four yards long. After
the "bride's garters" had been run for there came more
ribbons, silk kerchiefs, &c. Sometimes the women ran races
for tea.

A few years ago a farmer living at Middlewood, Oughti-
bridge, near Sheffield, wished to marry his housekeeper. So
he and the housekeeper went out one day and got two men
to act as witnesses. They all went together to the farmer's
house, but before they got there the farmer took the key of
the house-door from his pocket and gave it to the woman.
She unlocked the door and went into the house, locking the
door after her. After a time she unlocked it and allowed
her intended husband and the two witnesses to enter.* When
they had entered the farmer called upon the two men to
witness that he took the woman for his wife.

At Kneesall, in Nottinghamshire, there are two entrances
to the churchyard, one called the Bride Gate, and the other
the Corpse Gate.† On no account must the bride enter the
churchyard through the Corpse Gate.

When a corpse is carried to the churchyard it must be
carried with the feet foremost.

If you bake bread when there is a corpse in the house it
will not rise in the panchcon.

* By giving the key, and with it possession of the house, to the woman the
man seems to have been following the old Norse custom of purchasing a wife,
the delivery of possession of the house being the *mundr*, or consideration paid.

† *i.e.* lich-gate. No example of the word "bride-gate" occurs in the *New
Eng. Dict.*

When a corpse is laid out it should always be laid with the feet towards the rising sun.*

In Derbyshire it is said that people are buried with their feet towards the east because their feet will then point towards the Mount of Olives, upon which Christ will appear on the Day of Resurrection.

At Eckington, in the same county, when a corpse was laid out food was placed upon a table within reach of the body. This practice was invariably adhered to.

Never lock up and leave a house in which a corpse lies. When a death occurs the doors and windows of a house should be left open so that the spirit may pass out.

When a man is dying a long way off his image appears to his relations at the moment of death.

At Dore, in Derbyshire, it was customary when a corpse was laid out to lay a pewter plate containing a handful of salt upon the breast.†

At a funeral in Derbyshire wine is first offered to the bearers who carry the corpse. This custom is strictly maintained, the guests not receiving any wine until the funeral party has returned from church.

At Eyam, in the same county, it is considered unlucky for a man to be laid in the earth until some tears have been shed over him.

It is good that it should rain at a funeral, for if the dead man's friends are not mourning for him the heavens are weeping.

A man cannot die easily if he lie on hen's feathers.

When a dying man has "something on his mind" he cannot die until he has divulged it.

When you see a corpse do not come away without touching it, or you will have an ugly dream about it. In the East

---

* It was the custom of Christians to bury their dead with the feet towards the rising sun. The brass effigies and old sculptured figures in our English churches have their faces turned towards the east.

† The object was to keep the witch away, and we have just seen that salt in baptism was used for the same purpose.

Riding they say that you will never be afraid of the dead if you kiss the corpse.

The first person to meet a funeral will be the first to die. A woman living at Dronfield, in Derbyshire, was in the habit of following funerals to see who the first person to meet the corpse was.

As the spirit is leaving the body of one who is dying a rap is heard. This is called " spirit-rapping."

When you drink wine at a funeral every drop that you drink is a sin which the deceased has committed. You thereby take away the dead man's sins and bear them yourself.

At funerals in Dronfield the coffin is laid on a table, which is put outside the house, and covered with a white cloth. The neighbours come and lay flowers, such as bachelors' buttons, bergamot, &c., upon the cloth. They also sing a hymn.

In the East Riding people used to make their own shrouds, and this was often done many years before their deaths. In Derbyshire they often make their own coffins.

The spirit will always haunt the room in which its body died unless a candle be kept burning there all night.

When a corpse is taken from a house to be buried the door must remain open until the return of the mourners.

At all funerals in Eyam cakes were given to the mourners, and each mourner carried his cake to church wrapped up in a handkerchief. The cakes were always three-cornered or triangular, and were usually spiced with currants. The mourners also partook of spiced ale, which was known as " burnt drink." It was a dark-looking liquid, with a strongly aromatic smell, and consisted of ale spiced with cloves, nutmeg, ginger, and mace. It was drunk out of a large tankard, which was handed round to the mourners at the door of the house, when the funeral procession was about to start for the church. At the same time the three-cornered cakes were handed round to the mourners in a large round willow basket. The same tankard and basket were used at all funerals. The mourners walked before the corpse, and sang all the way to church.

At the funeral of one Lydia Brushfield every child in the village received a twopenny-piece and a cake.

At Eyam the corpse was watched all night, and a candle burnt all night at each end of the coffin. This watching was called "lich-waking." *

In Eyam, at the funeral of an unmarried girl, a garland made of white satin ribbons was carried before the corpse to church. The garland was laid on two crossed sticks of green willow, and was borne by four girls dressed in white.

When a corpse from another parish is buried in the church or churchyard of Eyam the passing-bell is not tolled on the · day of the funeral, but on the day before, and usually at twelve o'clock at noon.

At all funerals a portion of the "burnt drink" and three-cornered cakes was offered to the bees of the deceased.

It was the custom in Derbyshire for people to preserve their teeth in jars until their deaths, after which the teeth were put into their coffins and buried with them. Mothers would also preserve the teeth of their infant children and keep them in jars. It is said that when you go to heaven you will have to account for all the teeth that you have had upon earth. A man said that his grandmother used to call out at a funeral, "Have you got his teeth in the coffin?" or "Don't bury him without his teeth."

In the north of Derbyshire, when a young unmarried woman is buried, eight girls, dressed in white, who have been her friends, carry the body to church. They must always go by the main road, and not by a bye road. If they have to pass a chapel or other "place of worship," which she has been accustomed to attend, they stop and sing a hymn.

In the same county it was formerly the custom on All Saints' Day to strew flowers on the graves of one's relations

---

* Chaucer mentions the *lichwake*.

and friends. It is said that this day is especially sacred to the saints who have gone before, and that we should devote that day entirely to thinking of the departed.

It is lucky to be buried in linen. At funerals in the East Riding fifty years ago the woman wore black silk hoods with a long piece of silk hanging over their shoulders. These could be hired from dressmakers. When a young girl died she was carried to her grave by young girls who were her friends. These girls wore black frocks, white silk shawls, white gloves, and white bonnets. A woman's wardrobe was not considered complete if it did not contain a white silk shawl.

XI.—LOCAL AND CEREMONIAL CUSTOMS.

IT is the custom in Nottinghamshire to make the last sheaf of the harvest big in order to ensure a good crop the next year. The youngest boys in the village ride home on the last load of wheat, the wagon being decorated with branches of trees. Apples and buckets of cold water are thrown over the boys as they ride home singing the following harvest song :

> Mr. —— is a good man,
> He lets us ride his harvest home,
> He gives us apples, he gives us ale,
> We wish his heart may never fail.

> (Chorus) With a hip, hip, hurrah,
> A dry wagon, a dry wagon,
> A sup of cold water
> To keep it from swagging.

> God bless these horses that trail us home,
> For they've had many a weary bone,
> They've rent their clothes and torn their skin,
> All for to get this harvest in.

> (Chorus as before.)

In the East Riding of Yorkshire they sang:

> We ivver, we ivver at oor toon end,
> Hev a cup o' good yall, an' a croon to spend ;
> We've rent our cloos, we've tore oor skin,
> To get oor maister's harvest in.

A woman must always bind at least one sheaf in the field at harvest, and she must come to do this if she is ever so busy.

It is believed that the harvest will not be good unless a woman has had a hand in it. For the same reason a woman must always assist in the setting or planting of potatoes.

In the East Riding a young girl decked with ribbons and ears of wheat rode home on the last load of wheat.

When children at school make oaths or promises to each other the deponent wets his finger and shows it to the other children in order that they may see that it is wet. As soon as the finger is dry the deponent draws it across his throat like a knife and says:

> Is it wet ? Is it dry ?
> I'll cut my throat before I die.
> Here's the knife to cut it with,
> And here's the dish to catch the blood.*

Some people in Derbyshire take oaths on salt instead of on the Bible.

"In the time of roses," says one of my correspondents, "many a swain who had been disdained was the recipient of a white rose, well peppered, from a not too susceptible fair one."

At Cold-Aston, in Derbyshire, a young man was forsaken by his mistress, who married another. On the morning after the marriage large oval garlands made of evergreens, dragon lilies, and other flowers, and ribbons were found hung up in a tree near the forsaken lover's house. An onion and a bottle containing urine were also suspended from the tree. The tree was an old sycamore maple which formerly stood opposite to the

---

* "The emigrants from Salzburg dipped a wetted finger in salt and swore." Grimm's *Teut. Myth.*, p. 1049.

village blacksmith's shop. The same custom has been observed at Eyam within the last few years.

In Derbyshire a ceremony called " the ribbon-dance " is, or was, performed—I could not ascertain on what day. A pole is fixed up, from the top of which a number of long ribbons, each of a different colour, are hung. Each dancer takes a ribbon in his hand, and the dance is performed in such a way that the ribbons are twisted or woven into a particular shape, and afterwards untwisted. The performance is said to be a very pretty sight.

It is said that Woodend farm, now in the liberty of Beauchief, and county of Derby, was alienated from the adjoining parish of Norton in the following manner. A man being found dead on the farm the inhabitants of Beauchief requested the people of Norton to bury him in their churchyard, but they refused. A like application was made to the inhabitants of the adjacent hamlet of Ecclesall, but they also refused. After this the body was brought to Beauchief and buried in the abbey yard, and it is said that the inhabitants of Beauchief thereby acquired the right to include Woodend farm within their liberty. It is also said that the union of the hamlet of Upperthorpe with Sheffield occurred in the same way.

When a servant-girl first comes into a house she counts the number of the bars in the grate of the kitchen-fire, and also the number of steps on the stairs, and the cellar-steps.*

 I am told that when the bounds of a parish were beaten children were sometimes whipped to make them remember the occasion. The punishment of an offending boy was often reserved, it is said, by his father for this occasion. On the day of perambulation he got a good whipping.

A child should have an egg given to it when it first goes into a house. At Cold-Aston, in Derbyshire, when a child is taken into a house for the first time it is presented with an egg, a little salt, and a silver coin. The palm of the child's hand is crossed with the silver coin for luck. If it grasps the coin it

---

* Perhaps this is hardly folklore, but I give it the benefit of the doubt.

will have a good chance of living and thriving. Sometimes a pair of shoes and a silver sixpence are given, with a wish that the child's footsteps may be silvered through life with happiness.

When a man comes home drunk he throws his hat into the house to see whether he will be welcome. If the hat is taken into the house he will be welcome, but not if it is thrown out.

A cinder is regarded as an emblem of love. A cinder is sometimes wrapped up in a piece of paper and given to the object of one's affection. People are quite serious in making this present.

Always wash your hands before eating. Unless you do this you do not pay a proper respect to the giver of the food. Some people are very particular about this, not as a matter of cleanliness, but in deference to religious custom.

About ten years ago a new bell at Holmesfield, near Dronfield, in Derbyshire, was baptised.

It was usual to save money for making tharf-cakes. People would subscribe so much each, say a halfpenny a week, towards a fund for making these cakes. The cakes were eaten in November, first at one man's house, and the next year at another man's house. Thus the neighbours in their turn held a little yearly feast. These entertainments were called "tharf-cake joinings." At the thar-cake, or tharf-cake joining in Hathersage it was customary to keep a bit of the cake from one November to the next.

In Nottinghamshire it is said that a long time ago a lady who had lost her way on the heath was enabled to retrace her steps to the village in which she lived by the sound of the church bells. To show her gratitude for this she left an acre of ground to the sexton on condition that the bell should be rung at five in the morning and eight in the evening from October 19 to March 25. A similar tale is current in Sheffield. It relates that a man who had lost his way on the moors was saved by the sound of the bells in Sheffield church steeple. He, too, according to the popular account, left money or land for the ringing of bells in Sheffield church every Tuesday evening. "This Tuesday ringing is only in the winter months. It begins on

K

the Tuesday after Doncaster races—rather a curious calendar for church bells—and continues until Shrove Tuesday. It is, no doubt, an immemorial custom, connected possibly with the market-day." * At Ashover, in Derbyshire, the curfew bell used to be rung at eight in the evening from March to October, except on Saturday and Sunday, when it was rung at seven. It was not rung in the summer months at all.† There is a legend at Stamford Bridge, in the East Riding, about a man who lost his way when returning from a fair, and was saved by the sound of the bells. He left a guinea a year to the church for ever.

At Eyam, in Derbyshire, the curfew bell is rung at eight o'clock in the evening, from the 29th of October to the 25th of March. It is rung on a particular bell in the belfry. Immediately after the curfew bell has been rung the day of the month is tolled. This bell is there held up as a terror to children. A mother will say to her child, "If thou doesn't get off to bed th' curfew wi' th' iron teeth will come and fetch thee." At Treeton, near Sheffield, there is a field called Church Land, or Bell Field, "the income of which was paid to the bellman at the church for ringing the bell three times a day—at six, twelve, and eight o'clock." The bell-ringers have received the income for the last forty or fifty years. The size of the field is 2a. 1r. 20p. "All attempts to discover the origin of the charity have failed." ‡

I have heard people say that, fifty years ago and more, there was much rivalry in Derbyshire between one village and another. The inhabitants of one village, especially boys, would regard those living in an adjacent village as foreigners. If a boy went into another village he would be attacked by the boys living there, and I have been stoned myself when going through a village to which I did not belong. I have heard old people

---

* Leader's *Reminiscences of Old Sheffield*, 1875, p. 49.

† This was told to me by an aged woman at Ashover whose father was parish clerk early in the present century. She had often rung the bell herself.

‡ Charity Commission Inquiry, reported in *Sheffield Independent*, March 8, 1894.

say how much manners are improved in this respect. There was great rivalry between the boys of Dore and Totley, who used to revile each other, the Dore boys saying:

> Totley bugs,*
> Water-clogs,
> Water-porridge and hardly that.

The Totley boys replied:

> Dore bugs,
> Water-clogs,
> Eating out o' swill-tubs,
> Up a ladder and down a wall,
> A penny loaf will serve you all.

The girls of the two hamlets were equally hostile to each other, and used a set of verses, too coarse to quote, in which they imputed gross unchastity to each other. I have been told that people in Dore objected to live in houses which had chambers or staircases in them, and hence the line

> Up a ladder and down a wall

was intended to be a piece of stinging abuse.

Old Moses B——, of Dore, used to go up into his bedroom by means of pegs driven into the wall.

The inhabitants of Dore and Totley were very clannish. It was said that there were not more than three or four surnames amongst them, the saying being "Dore for Taylors and Elliots" (pronounced Yellots), and "Wards and Greens for Totley." Occasionally, to prevent confusion, a man took his wife's name. At one time there were not less than four persons in Dore who had adopted their wives' surnames.

When two boys are going to fight, an umpire is chosen to see fair play done. When the umpire has been agreed upon, he puts the back of his hand under the chin of one of the combatants and says, "Spit o'er my hand." He then puts his hand

---

* The word *bug* here means a hobgoblin or scarecrow, as in Coverdale's translation of Psalm xci. 5: "Thou shalt not nede to be afrayd for eny bugges by night." In More's *Comfort against Tribulation*, quoted in the *New Eng. Dict.*, mention is made of "such black bugges in dede as folk call douilles."

under the other boy's chin and repeats the same words. That having been done, he says :

> T' best cock
> Gie t' other a knock,

and then the fight begins.

When two boys quarrel and a fight is likely to ensue, one of them strikes the other on the shoulder with his fist three times, calling the first blow "the scarding blow," the second "the fighting blow," and the third "the everlasting blow." If his opponent, after having been struck three times, refuses to give battle, the other spits over his head and says, "T' cock o'er t' midden."

In Derbyshire, when cattle, such as horses and cows, die, it is usual to bury them under fruit-bearing trees in the orchard.

When people go into a new house they hold a feast, called a "house-warming," and drink hot ale till late at night.

The following account of a custom of swimming for a hamlet or village has been given to me. The hamlet of Pleasley Hill, situate in the parish of Mansfield and county of Nottingham, is divided from the ancient parish of Pleasley, in Derbyshire, by a deep, narrow ravine of limestone. Through this valley runs a stream or river, called the Mayden, or Meden, which separates Pleasley Hill from Pleasley. My informant says that a dispute once arose as to whether Pleasley Hill belonged to Mansfield or to Pleasley, and the matter was settled by a swimming match down the river. A Pleasley Hill man was chosen to represent his own hamlet, and a Pleasley man to represent that village. The swimmers, however, reached the goal at the same time, so that the Pleasley men did not succeed in getting Pleasley Hill annexed to their village. It still remains in the parish of Mansfield and in another county.*

At Bradwell, and other villages in the Peak of Derbyshire, young men who courted girls residing outside the limits of their

---

* The old woman from whom this information was derived said that her father was the man chosen to swim for Pleasley. This is evidently an interesting relic of a clan feud, like the feuds which have been continued down to recent times at Scarborough, Ludlow, Derby, Ashbourne, &c. See Mr. Gomme's *Village Community*, p. 240.

own township had to pay a fine, called "cock-walk," or "foot-ale," to the young men in whose township such girls resided. This fine was 1s. 6d. at Bradwell; in some places it was 1s. If the fine was paid, the interloper was permitted to go free and unmolested. But if the interloper refused to pay, a halter was put round his neck and he was driven round the village. The money was divided by the young men who exacted the fine, and it was usually spent in drink.

It is the custom in East Yorkshire for girls to give a silver coin to the men working in a hay-field or harvest-field, when they first enter the field. Unless they do this the men are privileged to kiss them.

When a man's bees swarm they can be followed upon his neighbour's property by tinkling a bell, an old tin shovel, a pan, &c. The bees are said to like this noise, and the tinkling gives the owner of the swarm the right to follow it. In the evening before they swarm they make a peculiar murmur, like " ootie, ootie, ootie."

In East Yorkshire it is said that a man must be able to keep the pot boiling on Sunday before he marries, by which is meant that he must be able to provide a home for a wife. The pot is a large iron cauldron, called "t' keeal pot," suspended by a "rackan hook" from a beam or bar, called the "galley balk," in which meat, vegetables, and flour dumplings are boiled together, the broth being served in large basins for dinner. Sunday is known as "pot-day," Monday as "pudding-day," Tuesday as "pie-day," Wednesday as "pot-day," Thursday as "pudding-day," Friday as "pie-day"; on Saturday odds and ends of all sorts are eaten up.

A man at Cold-Aston, in Derbyshire, took an oath that if he did not shoot the gamekeeper he hoped all his hair would come off.* Eventually his hair did come off, and it was said that it was on account of the oath.

* My informant said that he had no hair at all on his head; "it looked like a bladder of lard." Vows neither to cut or comb the hair until an enemy had been slain or a comrade avenged were common amongst the ancient Germans. See *Tacit. Germ.*, 31, and references in Vigfusson and Powell's *Corpus Poet. Boreale*, i. 424.

XII.—FAIRIES, GIANTS, DWARFS, AND GHOSTS.

THERE are people in Derbyshire who firmly believe that giants and dwarfs were real beings which once existed in England. In that county fairies are said to be "little beings about a yard high which are always jumping up and down."

The rings which fairies make on the ground cannot be removed by the plough. They appear in every kind of field but cornfields, where they do not appear.

When people are lost on the moors they sometimes see fairies dancing before them and leading them on their way.

Wherever the fairies dance the green ring or dark earth is always to be seen. The fairies can always be seen, in the dusk of evening, in a certain meadow called the Stocking Field, at Calver, near Baslow, in Derbyshire. They dance in rings, and in the midst of the ring is a little woman, herself a fairy, who is called the midwife, and is always blindfolded.*

In Derbyshire, when a woman is about to be delivered of a child, the fairies come, nobody knows how, bringing with them a little fairy woman, called a midwife, whose eyes are covered with a hood. In the same mysterious manner as the fairies bring the midwife they fetch her away, after she has assisted the woman in her labour.†

A man said that when he was a boy he saw a fairy sitting on the stone steps which led up to a bedroom in an old house, and was much frightened at the apparition. She appeared to be a diminutive woman.

Fairies are always dressed in a red mantle and hood, which covers the whole body, and witches are dressed exactly in the same manner.

---

* The man who related this account to me firmly believed it, and he said, " What a shame it is that the midwife should be blindfolded and not see the fun that goes on ! "

† Here the fairy midwife appears as Juno Lucina, goddess of child-birth, the attendant fairies forming her escort or train. Amongst the Greeks birth was forwarded by divine beings called 'Ειλείθυιαι, handmaids of Hera. See *Iliad*, xi. 270.

If a fairy does you a kindness, or a " good turn," you must keep it secret. If you tell anybody the fairy will never do you a good turn again.

A Derbyshire man described dwarfs to me as " very small pretty-featured people," who run about in the chinks and fissures of rocks. A tale is told in the High Peak about a man who went to see the end of the world. He kept going down and down in the earth until he came to the place where these little people dwelt. He said " They were no bigger than cocks and hens."

Women at Eckington, in Derbyshire, used to sweep their hearths up clean every night before they went to bed. They said that unless they did this the fairies would never visit their houses and bring them good things.

Many years ago a woman, who lived at Morewood's* Farm, near Holmesfield, in Derbyshire, went away from home to her daughter's funeral. Although she left the house empty and locked up, yet when she came back she found that the fire was still burning and the house put in order. She believed that the fairies had done this, and the affair was a good deal talked about.

Mountain-flax is spun by the fairies.

A part of a road leading out of Crowle, in Lincolnshire, is unfinished, and never will be finished. A farmer once met a mysterious person † who inquired of him why the road was not finished, and told the farmer that he would finish it if he would turn his back and not watch how it was done. But when the farmer heard the tinkering and hammering on the road he could not resist the temptation of looking round. He then saw a number of little men working at the road. But they vanished in an instant, and the road returned to its former condition and never can be mended.

In Derbyshire women used to mix their leaven for oatcake the night before baking it. In the night they heard the voices

---

* Pronounced *Murruds* by my informant.

† This appears to be Robin Goodfellow in the character of *lar vialis*, or tutelary god of the ways. Some describe the mysterious person as " a man in black."

of "little people" pattering about the house and moving the "doshin," or bowl in which the leaven was mixed, about.

It is said that fairies come into grocers' shops and take away anything that they may fancy. If the grocer, or any of his family, come into the shop whilst the fairies are there, they are blindfolded by the motion of the fairies' hands.

Fairies sometimes take babies away. They take a healthy and leave a sickly child.

It is said that Dead Man's Lane, Ecclesall, near Sheffield, was frequented by fairies. The lane was overgrown with grass, upon which, it is said, the dark green fairy rings could be seen.

At Curbar, in Derbyshire, it is said that Morris dancing is really fairy dancing, and that "Morris dancing" means "fairy dancing." * Morris dancers of the present day, it is said, go through the same form of dancing that the fairies go through, except that they cannot perform such intricate figures as the fairies can. The figures which the Morris dancers of the present day go through are very elaborate and very difficult to learn. A man said to me that Morris dancing had been "taken away from the fairies." Morris dancing is still practised at Eyam and at Tideswell, in Derbyshire, and the following is the tune which the dancers use :

* This connection between Morris dancing and fairy dancing is very curious. Some fields in Norton, in Derbyshire, are called Morris Lands, and I have seen them mentioned in a document of the sixteenth century.

When the dancers get to the long note they throw up their handkerchiefs. They have a red or blue handkerchief in one hand, and a white one in the other.

People in Lincolnshire say that a "Dead Cart" comes round in the middle of the night, drawn without horses or any visible means of locomotion. If you look out of the window when you hear the noise of its wheels passing by you will see yourself in the cart amongst those who are doomed to die in the coming year. A death will happen in the house on or before the third day after the cart has been heard.

Cross-roads are often said to be haunted by barghasts, boggards, or headless women. Thus "the boggard of Bunting Nook" (a place in Norton, near Sheffield, where three roads meet) is held up as a terror to children, and a headless woman is said to appear at the place where three roads meet between Cold-Aston and Dronfield, in Derbyshire. It is said that a headless woman used to be seen between Bowshaw and Hullat Hall, in Dronfield parish.

Wherever there is a "four lane ends," or place where two roads cross each other, a ghost is to be seen at night.

A barghast is described as a being which resembles a large black dog, having eyes like saucers. One of these beings is said to have appeared at "three lane ends"* at Bury Hill, near Holmesfield. A woman who saw a barghast near these "three lane ends" said that it was invisible to her sister, who died a month afterwards.

If you see a barghast it will be visible to your companions if you touch them.

In the night-time people who lie in bed sometimes hear the sounds of cock-crowing in the house downstairs when there are no cocks near.

A headless woman is said to appear at midnight at an old house situate at Over Hurst, in the parish of Hathersage, in Derbyshire.

People sometimes say that they see headless dogs, and that the appearance of such a dog is an omen of death.

* *Trivium.*

Near Dead Lane, or, as it was formerly called, Deadman's Lane, near Greystones, Ecclesall, in the parish of Sheffield, a headless woman robed in white is said to appear.

"Peggy wi' t' lantern" is usually seen "in sicks or marshy places."

On a common between Ossington and Kneesall, in Nottinghamshire, a ghost in the form of a woman appears after sunset. This being is called Peggy Whooper.

The ghost of one of the Brights of Whirlow Hall, near Sheffield, was said to appear in a lane near the house in the shape of a black bird with a white tail or wing. Sometimes it was felt, but not seen, as in the case of a man from Dore, who, returning home late one evening on the back of his ass, was lifted from his seat in the deepest part of the lane, and fixed upright in the middle of the lane, the ass going on as if nothing had happened. He was paralysed with fear and unable to move until the spirit allowed him to proceed.

At a house in Rotherham it is said that a headless woman appears at midnight. She walks downstairs carrying her own head under her arm.*

A tale is told in Derbyshire about a mother whose daughter had died, and who was so overcome with grief that she could not be persuaded to go to bed for eleven weeks. At the end of that time her daughter appeared to her and said, "Mother, if you grieve for me thus I cannot rest in the kingdom of heaven." After this the care-worn mother dried up her tears and ceased to lament.

The Devil is always in our midst at twelve o'clock, the hour of midnight.

If a ghost appears, and you say to it, "In the name of the Lord, why visitest thou me?" it will tell you what it has come for.

It is said that the following spectres used to be seen on the common at Cold-Aston, in Derbyshire. First, three tall, thin women, standing in a line, with three hour-glasses in their

---

* Compare the story of St. Denys, who, when beheaded, took up his own head in his hands.

hands ;* secondly, a tall man, three yards high, with an oak tree over his shoulder ; thirdly, a man with a scythe over his shoulder. The man who, as he alleged, saw these things on the common said that the appearance of the woman with the hour-glasses meant that such or such a person had not more than three hours to live ; the giant with the oak tree came, he said, to tell whether that person was young or old ; the man with the scythe came to cut him down. In the appearance or vision which my informant mentioned, the oak tree was a young one, indicating that the man who was about to die was young.

It is said that ghosts have been seen recently in the same village. A very small, wizzened old woman was seen by several people. She was usually found sitting against a wall, and when spoken to she vanished. A girl was much frightened one even-ing by seeing a white bird, resembling a goose, but covered with wings. She practised the spell of walking round it nine times, when it vanished. Another person saw a white calf at the very moment when her friend was dying.

About 1840 the parish clerk of Norton, in Derbyshire, and his apprentice went to play the organ, then standing in the west gallery of the church. The apprentice, whose face was turned towards the nave of the church, told the clerk that he could see a woman sitting alone in one of the high cloth-covered pews, and that he believed she was spectral. Thereupon they both rushed frantically down the steps, which were very tortuous and awkward. The clerk would never again play the organ in church in the dusk of evening.

At Sleaford, in Lincolnshire, a man's wife being suddenly taken ill, he borrowed a horse and rode off for the doctor. As he rode he noticed that on one side of his horse he could see the ground with wonderful clearness ; it was so bright that he could have seen a pin. But on the other side of the horse it was so dark that he could not even see his own foot. By this he knew that his wife would die.

---

* Evidently the Parcae or Norns. Instead of the distaff or the threads of life they carry hour-glasses.

At a lonely house near Stony Middleton, in Derbyshire, the ghost of a murdered woman is said to appear by night, and make holes in the loaves of bread in the house. One night the master and mistress of the house, who were bakers, sat up in order that they might see her. They did not see her, but the holes were made in the loaves just as before. The holes were so large that the loaves could not be sold.

At Highlow Hall, near Hathersage, it is said that a man dressed in white, and riding on a white horse, appears at midnight.

About midnight on New Year's Eve a man at Eckington, in Derbyshire, said that he saw a spectre in the shape of a wild white horse. The colliers in this neighbourhood say that they often see this white horse.

A woman in Nottinghamshire used to see a spectral white calf in the village where she lived. She said that she could see it because she was born at twilight, and so had the power of seeing what others could not see.

In Nottinghamshire there was once a poor woman who died from neglect in giving birth to a child, and her husband married the midwife who ought to have attended her but neglected to do so. The spirit of the dead woman haunted the midwife's cottage for a long time, but at last it was "laid" in a box by a clergyman and buried therein. Thirty years afterwards some workmen broke open the box in which the spirit was laid. It then made such a noise that they thought the house was falling down, and ran away from their work in a fright.

Many people believe that spirits are always flying about in the air, and that you ought to be careful how you shut a door or a window lest you hurt them by so doing.

It is said of a man who was imprisoned for poaching, that the spirits of the birds which he had shot used to appear outside the prison-bars and peck at the windows.

In the East Riding of Yorkshire a spirit which gives warning before death is known as a "fetch."

To exorcise spirits repeat these lines :

Jesus, a name high over all,
O'er earth, and air, and sea,
Before thy name the angels fall,
And devils fear and flee.

XIII.—FIRST-FRUITS AND SACRIFICE.

COLLIERS in the north of Derbyshire leave a hundredweight of coal in the pit every week for the fairies.

People at Curbar in Derbyshire used to set bowls of cream on the hill-tops where they thought that the fairies mostly dwelt. The cream was always drunk, but the fairies were never seen.

When people gather bilberries, blackberries, or other fruit, it is usual in Derbyshire to throw the first bilberry, or other fruit gathered, over one's head, and to say, "Pray God send me good luck to-day."

When you taste the first fruit of any season, such as an apple or a gooseberry, you should wish something, and your wish will be granted.

When you buy or hire a piece of land, the first thing to be done is to take a spade full of earth, throw it up in the air, and catch it on the back of your spade. Unless you do this your crops will not thrive. When a man has ill luck with his crops somebody will say to him, " Ah, thah didn't turn t' spade round."

When you plant beans, potatoes, or other fruit in single rows, you must begin the row by setting two beans, or two potatoes, or as the case may be. In like manner, when you begin to sow, if you unintentionally drop a handful of seeds, you must not pick them up, but let them remain where they are. Unless you do this the crop will not thrive.

A cow having cast her calf at Hazelbarrow, in the parish

of Norton, in Derbyshire, the dead body was wrapped in straw, and a bonfire made of it in the middle of the farm-yard. All the other cows in the cowhouses were then driven round the blazing pile. It was said that the smell of the roasting calf would prevent the other cows from casting their calves.*

XIV.—PROVERBS AND LOCAL RIMES.

A DERBYSHIRE mile is said to be measured with a dead cat and a listing cap.

If one offers you his left hand to shake, it is usual to say to him, " The left hand for a rogue."

A loquacious person is said to have " as much jaw as a sheep's head."

When a child is cocksure of anything, he will sometimes say, " I'm sure and certain, burnt to death."

Always burn your hair when you cut it off, or the birds will carry it away.

When one has made a witty remark it is usual to give him a button, and to say to him, " You've won the button."

Those who have sold themselves to the Devil will always have plenty of money.

Of ill-gotten wealth it is said, " What comes under the Devil's belly will be sure to go over his back."

When you are married you have tied a knot with your tongue which you cannot unloosen with your teeth.

In the East Riding they say, " A bletherin' coo soon forgets her calf," meaning that excessive grief does not last long.

> March winds and May sun
> Make clothes white and maids dun.

Two neighbours having quarrelled, one of them said to the other, " I hope I shall live to see thy coffin walk."

* See the Introduction to my *Sheffield Glossary*, p. xx.

In Yorkshire they say that lazy people move as if dead flies crawled off them.

When you spill salt you must drop a tear for every grain that you spill.

People in South Yorkshire say that when Mary Queen of Scots was beheaded one of the bystanders struck her fallen head with his hand, when she turned up her eyes and blushed. This is often told to children by nurses and servants.

When one asks for the best of anything people say, " You are like the bishop : the best will do for me."

There is an old saying :

> A pin a day,
> A groat a year.

People say :

> A nip for new,
> And a bite for blue.

In Derbyshire they say :

> My coat's as black as pitch,
> Say the bells of Hather-sitch.

I believe the first line of this couplet is intended to represent the jingle of the bells. Hathersage, it may be noted, is sometimes pronounced Hather-sedge.

In the East Riding of Yorkshire they say, " If you mind your own business, and let other people's business alone, you will get a mill at Howden." They also say that " What is to be will be, if mountains are in the way ; if it is not to be, mole-hills will stop it."

To a talkative person one will say, " You've a tongue like a lamb's tail ; it's always wagging."

The following lines are heard in North Derbyshire :

> Baslow for gentlefolk,
> Calver for trenchers,
> Middleton for rogues and thieves,
> And Eyam for pretty wenches.

The people of Calver are said to be great gluttons.

Between Monsal Dale and Ashford the following lines are heard :

> The piper of Shacklow,
> The fiddler of Finn ;
> The old woman of Demon's Dale
> Calls them all in.*

In the East Riding, when a man is vexed, he will say, " It is enough to vex a saint in a stone wall."

One who anticipates difficulty is told not to cross the bridge till he gets to it.

When people hear the thunder they say that God is speaking to the wicked.

A cross child is said to have come from under a crab tree.

If a man is very dirty people sometimes say, " He's as black as the Old Lad's nutting-bag."

A turned-up nose indicates deceit.

The following lines are said in Derbyshire concerning places in that county :

> Ashford in the water,
> Bakewell in the spice,
> Sheldon in the nutwood,
> Longstone in the lice.

At Norton Free School, in Derbyshire, all the boys had to say the following lines every Friday morning :

> If well thou art rise soon each day,
> First praise thy God, then to Him pray,
> And wash thyself both clean and neat,
> And as you come if you should meet
> Some boys that play, don't waste your time
> As they do, for it is a crime.
> But leave the boys, come straight to school,
> And there sit still ; be not a fool.
> No talk, no play, but mind your task,
> And chief of those you'll be at last.

---

* The Ordnance map gives the last-named place as " Dimins Dale." Compare the surname Dimsdale. Witches " often take a piper to their meetings, whose business is to play to their feasting and dancing." (Grimm's *Teutonic Myth.*, p. 1046.) Dimins Dale reminds one of Dimons Bay in Iceland, mentioned in Eyrbyggia Saga.

The following lines are sometimes written on the fly-leaves of books :

> If thou art borrowed by a friend,
> Right welcome shalt thou be
> To read, to study, not to lend,
> But to return to me.
>
>   *   *   *   *
>
> [Christopher Johnson] is my name,
> And England is my nation,
> [Cold-Aston] is my dwelling-place,
> And Christ is my salvation.
> When I am dead and in my grave,
> And all my bones are rotten,
> Take up this book and in it look,
> When I am quite forgotten.

THE HORSE'S PRAYER.

> Going up the hill whip me not,
> Coming down the hill hurry me not,
> On level ground spare me not,
> Loose in the stable forget me not,
> Of hay and and corn rob me not,
> Of clean water stint me not,
> With sponge and water neglect me not,
> Of soft dry bed deprive me not,
> Tired and hot wash me not,
> If sick or cold chill me not,
> With bit or rein O jerk me not,
> And when you are angry strike me not.

The following song was formerly sung in the south of Yorkshire, and is well remembered by old people. I have entitled it

THE LOVERS.*

> He stepped up to a cottage door,
> A pretty maid stepped o'er the floor,
> And she cried out aloud " Who's there ? "
> And she cried out aloud " Who's there ? "
>
> " It hails, it rains, it snows, it blows,
> And I am wet through all my clothes,
> So I pray thee, love, let me in,
> So I pray thee, love, let me in."

* From Crookes, near Sheffield.

She said " Kind sir, that ne'er can be,
There's nobody in the house but me,
And I dare not let thee in,
And I dare not let thee in.

" My father and mother are fast asleep,
My brother's gone out to tend his sheep,
And I dare not let thee in,
And I dare not let thee in."

He turned him round elsewhere to go,
But kind compassion she did show,
And she called him back again,
And she called him back again.

They spent that night in sweet content,
And the very next day to the church they went
And he made her his charming bride,
And he made her his charming bride.

THE LADY'S GLOVE.*

A wealthy young squire from Tanswick he came
A-courting a nobleman's daughter so fair ;
All for to marry her was his intent,
All friends and relations had given consent.

The time was appointed for their wedding-day,
A young farmer was chosen to give her away ;
No sooner did the lady the farmer espy
It enragèd her heart : " O my heart," she did cry.

Instead of being married she took to her bed,
The thought of the farmer so ran in her head ;
Coat, waistcoat, and breeches the fair maid put on,
And she went a-shooting with her dog and gun.

She oftentime firèd, but nothing she killed,
Till at length the young farmer came into the field.
" I thought thou hadst been at the wedding," she cried,
" To wait on the squire and give him his bride."

" O, no," said the farmer, with his heart full of love,
" I ne'er could give her away, I love her too well !"
The lady was pleasèd to hear him so bold,
And gave him her glove all flowerèd with gold.

---

* From the East Riding. It seems to be a corrupt fragment of a fine poem.

Returning home she made a vow only to marry the man who found her glove, and said :

*   *   *   *   *   *

> " The man that shall find it and bring it to me
> The bride of that man and his wife will I be."

A NURSERY RIME.

> There was a man who had a lad ;
> He put him in a pea swad.
> The pea swad it was so green ;
> He put him in a silver pin.*
> The silver pin it was so fine,
> He put him in a glass of wine.
> The glass of wine it was so good,
> He put him in a log of wood.
> The log of wood it was so thick,
> He put him in a candlestick.
> The candlestick it was so nasty,
> He put him in an apple pasty.
> The apple pasty was so hot,
> He put him in a porridge pot.
> The porridge pot it was so wide,
> He put him in an old house side,†
> And there he lived and there he died,
> And nobody either laughed or cried.

COUNTING OUT RIMES.

> Eena, meena, mina, mona,
> Jack the keena, kina, kona,
> Kaila, waila, kit . . . . laddie.
> Thou shalt be a soldier's laddy
> To drive a horse and beat the drum.
> O. U. T. spells out goes he.

---

* Probably the word was pronounced *peen*. See *peen end* in the supplement to my *Sheffield Glossary*, p. 43.

† The last three lines appear to have reference to "foundation sacrifice," or to the burial of a live child under or within the wall of a newly-built house as a sacrifice to the local deity. Compare a very different version in Halliwell's *Nursery Rhymes of England*, 1886, p. 203.

ANOTHER VERSION

Eena, meena, mina, mona,
Jack the jeena, jina, jona,
Ah me, count 'em along.
You shall be the soldier's man
To ride the horse, to beat the drum,
To tell the soldiers when to come,
One, two, three,
Out goes thee.

XV.—TWO PAGAN HYMNS.

THE two popular hymns which follow, like the carol which has already appeared in these pages,* contain a mixture of pagan and christian ideas. In the hymn beginning "Plenty of ale to-night, my boys," the pagan element predominates, and it will be seen that "the threble Thribers" are the three Norns, or Parcae, who foretold the destinies of men. A tradition respecting the appearance of these beings in a Derbyshire village has already been given in a previous section.† The first hymn is sung in the north of Derbyshire, and there are variants in other parts of England. The second hymn has been communicated to me by a friend, who informs me that it is sung at Stoke Prior. I have published and commented upon the first hymn elsewhere ‡ The second hymn is printed exactly as it was furnished to me, the two footnotes as to various versions being supplied by my informant. The hymns have no titles, and I number them consecutively.

(1)

Plen-ty of ale to-night, my boys, and then I will sing you!

---

* *Ante*, p. 108.   † *Ante*, p. 84.
‡ *Gentleman's Magazine*, July, 1890.

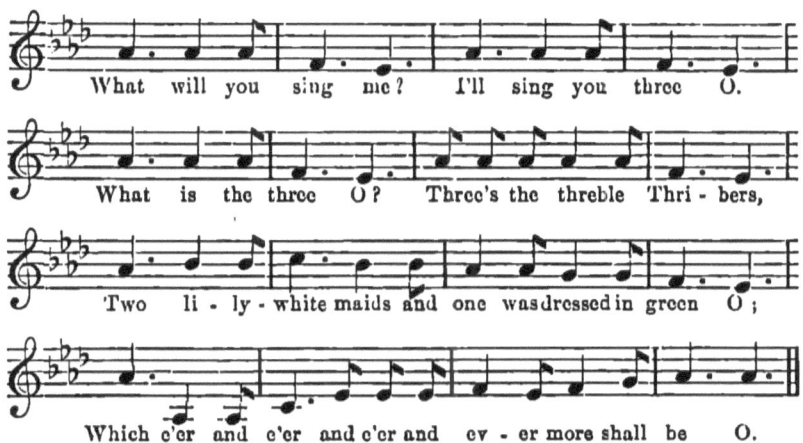

What will you sing me? I'll sing you three O.
What is the three O? Three's the threble Thri - bers,
Two li - ly - white maids and one was dressed in green O ;
Which e'er and e'er and e'er and ev - er more shall be O.

When this has been sung, another singer repeats the first two lines, but instead of saying " I'll sing you three O," he sings:

> I'll sing you twelve O.
> What is the twelve O ?
> Twelve is the twelve Apostles,
> Two lily-white maids and one was dressed in green O,
> Which e'er and e'er and e'er and evermore shall be O,

the last two lines serving as a chorus.

In this manner the following lines are repeated until the singer gets to the " threble Thribers," with which the song began :

> Twelve Apostles.
> Eleven Archangels.
> Ten Commandments.
> Nine Bright Shiners.
> Eight the Gabriel riders.
> Seven golden stars in heaven.
> Six came on the board.
> Five by water.
> Four Gospel rhymers.
> Three threble Thribers,*
> Two lily-white maids and
> One was dressed in green O.

---

* The *i* in " Thribers " is long.

(2)

1ST VERSE.

Sing, sing, and what shall we sing? Sing all ov - er one, And what was one?

One was God (to)* the righteous man, To save our souls to rest, A - men.

2ND VERSE.

Sing, sing, and what shall we sing? Sing all ov - er two, And what was two?

Two was the Jewry, One was God (to) the righteous man, To save our souls to rest, A-men.

3RD VERSE.

Sing, sing, and what shall we sing? Sing all ov - er three, And

what was three? Three was the Trin - i - ty, Two was the Jew - ry,

One was God the right-eous man, To save our souls to rest, A - men.

* *to* probably an error.

4TH VERSE.

Sing,	sing,	and what shall we sing?	Sing	all	ov - er	four,	And
Sing,	sing,	and what shall we sing?	Sing	all	ov - er	five,	And
Sing,	sing,	and what shall we sing?	Sing	all	ov - er	six,	And
Sing,	sing,	and what shall we sing?	Sing	all	ov - er	seven,	And
Sing,	sing,	and what shall we sing?	Sing	all	ov - er	eight,	And

what	was	four?	Four was the la-dy's bower,*Three was the Trin - i - ty, &c.
what	was	five?	Five was the man a - live, Four was the la-dy's bow'r,&c.
what	was	six?	Six was the cru - ci - fix, Five was the man a - live,&c.
what	was	seven?	Seven was the Bride of Heav'n, Six was the cru - ci - fix, &c.
what	was	eight?	Eight was the crooked straight,Seven was the Bride of Heav'n,&c.

* Lady's bower, lady bird, lady or lady's birth (?).

INDEX.

Printed by NICHOLS & SONS, 25, Parliament Street, Westminster.

www.ingramcontent.com/pod-product-compliance
Lightning Source LLC
Chambersburg PA
CBHW030546040726
47497CB00008B/2595